PLATIES
— AND —
SWORDTAILS

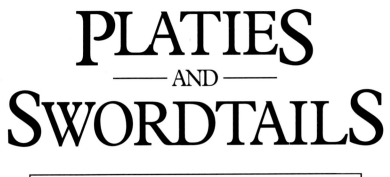

PLATIES
— AND —
SWORDTAILS

An Aquarist's Handbook

Derek and Pat Lambert

Series Editor: Derek Lambert

BLANDFORD

A Blandford Book
First published in the UK 1995
by Blandford
An imprint of Cassell plc
Wellington House
125 Strand
LONDON
WC2R 0BB

Distributed in the United States
by Sterling Publishing Co., Inc.
387 Park Avenue South, New York, NY 10016–8810

Distributed in Australia
by Capricorn Link (Australia) Pty Ltd
2/13 Carrington Road, Castle Hill, NSW 2154.

*A catalogue record for this book is available from
the British Library*

ISBN 0 7137 2368 8

Typeset by Cambrian Typesetters, Frimley, Surrey
Printed and bound in Spain

Contents

PICTURE CREDITS

Preface

This book has been written for a wide range of aquarists from the beginner to the very experienced. In it we have drawn together a mass of information from many different sources which, it is hoped, will give the reader a complete and up-to-date view of this fascinating group of fish.

Some of the information has been gathered from various scientific papers. These contain a wealth of information which has enabled me to add a depth and dimension to the work which would otherwise have been lacking. We are therefore very grateful to Jim Chambers of the Natural History Museum for all his aid over many years.

Many aquarists have, unknowingly, had some input into this book. Over the last 10 years we have regularly sat on information panels for specialist livebearer organizations and given lectures at aquarist gatherings. Whilst this has been quite hard work, it has also been very rewarding, because many aquarists have little nuggets of information which have proved to be extremely useful, so we would like to thank them all. All the practical information about aquarium care and breeding comes from first-hand personal experiences. If your experiences differ, well, we all know the fish don't read the books!

We are grateful to *Aquarian*, who kindly sponsored us on the Aquarian Endangered Species Expedition 1992. This field trip provided useful information about some of the *Xiphophorus* habitats we had not previously visited and helped establish the range of *X. clemenciae*.

There are 3 people who need a special mention.

John Dawes encouraged us to write our first article for an aquatic magazine. Without this encouragement we are sure this book would never have happened.

Dr Joanne Norton has shown us what is possible with cultivated fish and we just hope that, one day, we will be able to produce a cultivated strain that is as good as one of Joanne's.

The other person who needs a special thank-you is Jim Langhammer. His guidance and assistance over the past few years in many different ways has been invaluable to us.

We would also like to pay tribute to the 'Three Greats' of the Xiphophorin scientific community: Dr Myron Gordon, Dr Donn Eric Rosen and Dr Klaus D. Kallman. Between them they have been responsible for the naming of many of the fish in the genus *Xiphophorus*, have worked extensively with the living animal, and have increased our understanding of this fascinating group of fish a thousandfold.

Derek and Pat Lambert

Introduction

The hobby of aquarium-fish-keeping goes back to the late 1700s when Johann Matthaeus Bechstein (1757–1822) helped popularize the keeping of fish and plants from European waters. He became known as the father of the aquarium and vivarium but we feel sure he would be totally amazed at how popular this hobby has become. Millions of people in the UK now keep tropical fish and almost every sizeable town has an aquarium shop. Even where we live, in the middle of rural England, we have 2 aquarium shops within a 16 km radius of our house.

Since the early 1930s, when they were first introduced to the aquarium hobby, platies and swordtails have been one of the most popular groups of fish. Even the wild forms fulfilled the criteria needed to make a fish suitable for aquarium life, i.e. pleasing colour, small size, hardy, peaceful, and interesting breeding habits. However, once it became known that the various species could be crossed to create some quite spectacular hybrids, a whole new hobby took off. The art of cultivation was soon in full swing and many new colour varieties and several new fancy-finned forms became available.

In the late 1950s and early 1960s these cultivated varieties so dominated the livebearer scene that the wild forms had almost been forgotten by aquarists. However, the pendulum eventually swung back the other way, in part helped by a book written by Kurt Jacobs. This was entitled *Livebearing Aquarium Fishes* and, whilst the platies and swordtails shown were almost entirely of the cultivated types, due mention was given to the wild species which were almost unknown in the aquarium hobby.

The interest this book sparked amongst a few aquarists coincided with the advent of jet travel. Suddenly the world had become a whole lot smaller and some brave, hardy and outright foolish aquarists found that they could go to the native habitats and collect their own fish. In the UK, Howard Preston was the first of this new breed and, despite the problems and risks involved, managed to bring back a number of new species to the UK hobby.

In the early 1970s, several specialist livebearer clubs started around the world. These centred on Germany, the USA and the UK, and exchanges between these organizations took place on a regular basis. Ivan Dibble of the UK was by far and away the most active in this department and was responsible for the widespread circulation of many species.

In 1983 we went on our first field trip to Jamaica. At the time we were particularly interested in the genus *Gambusia* but, whilst examining one habitat, we caught some *Xiphophorus maculatus*. These fish were obviously commercial fish which had been introduced and had managed to gain a toe-hold in what was a very competitive habitat. Our next field trip was in 1986 and was to Mexico. We immediately fell in love with the country and people of this fascinating land and have since returned 6 times. During these visits we have been able to study the fish and their habitats in some depth. This information has been of vital importance in the preparation of this book because, quite often, it holds the key to success with a particularly difficult species.

In 1989 a new list of 'Fishes of North America, endangered, threatened, or of special concern' was published by the American Fisheries Society. In this were listed 364 species of fish from Canada, the USA and Mexico which required protection in the wild. This number had risen from 251 in the previous list published in 1979. *Xiphophorus couchianus*, *gordoni* and *meyeri* were included as endangered and *X. clemenciae* was listed as of special concern because of its limited habitat. When we were on the Aquarian Endangered Species Expedition in 1992, we were able to confirm that this species does have a much wider range than at first thought. However, the other 3 species are in serious trouble and it cannot be long before others have to be added.

One thing which has become abundantly clear over the years that we have been visiting Mexico is the phenomenal pace of development. Where one year there was a pond, the next year there is a new hotel or factory open and doing business. The Mexicans do care for their environment and are trying to prevent the loss of species as much as possible but, in a country where almost every lake, pond, ditch or river may hold a unique fish, it is inevitable that some will be lost.

In 1991 Dr Kallman of the Osborn Laboratories of Marine Sciences in New York was informed that his laboratory was being closed down due to lack of funds and the live *Xiphophorus* collection would have to be broken up. Dr Kallman decided to distribute many of the fish to the aquatic hobby, where, it was hoped, they would be maintained in the long term.

The role of aquarists in the long-term maintenance of endangered fish has yet to be fully worked out. Many scientists are very negative about the role they can play. Others, however, believe they may hold the key to the survival of many species. At present all the national livebearer aquatic societies operate species maintenance programmes to make sure species do not die out in the hobby, even if they do so in the wild.

In discussing the cultivated varieties and strains, we have deliberately avoided giving too much detail about the genetics of the fish concerned.

This is because, to be accurate, the full genetic background of the strain must be given and, although this is useful to the advanced breeder who is having a problem with a particular strain, it is confusing to many other aquarists. In Chapter 10, we decided to list the species in simple alphabetical order for several different reasons. From a scientific point of view, it might have been more appropriate to list them according to their species-groups, or even by their cladistic relationships, but this is a book written for aquarists, inexperienced as well as experienced, who might have difficulties in finding a species placed in this sort of scientific ordering. The only possible alternative would be to list the platies and swordtails separately but, once again, problems could arise from not knowing where a particular species would be listed. Having ourselves suffered, in the past, the frustrations of moving back and forth within a book to find a species, we have come to the conclusion that strict alphabetical order is simplest and best.

1
Classification

The genus *Xiphophorus*, to which the platies and swordtails belong, was erected by Heckel in 1848. He placed 3 species within the genus, 2 of which have now been moved to other genera (*Pseudoxiphophorus bimaculatus* and *Gambusia gracilis*). The genus *Platypoecilus* was erected by Gunther in 1866. In 1907 Regan showed that the supposedly significant differences in the structure of the teeth had no basis in fact. However, it was not until the gonopodial characteristics of the Poeciliidae were thoroughly studied by Regan in 1913 that the close relationship between these 2 genera was realized.

In 1913 Langer also analysed the anatomy of the gonopodia and their suspensoria in *X. helleri* and *Platypoecilus maculatus*. He saw many anatomical similarities and suggested combining the genera, but did not do so.

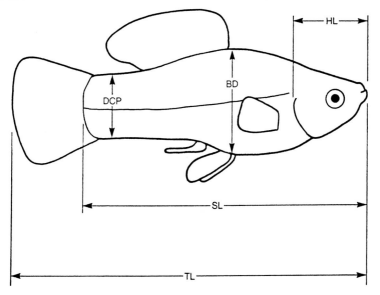

Fig. 1 Male *Xiphophorus variatus* showing important measurements used by scientists. BD: Body Depth. DCP: Depth of Caudal Peduncle. HL: Head Length. SL: Standard Length. TL: Total Length.

In 1924, this close relationship was once again noted by Carl Hubbs, who erected the tribe of Xiphophorini to contain them. In 1943, when Myron Gordon and Carl Hubbs described the new species *X. pygmaeus*, the similarities were once again noted and the new species assigned to the older genus in anticipation of the combining of the 2 genera. Finally, in 1951, after 38 years of prevarication and doubt, Myron Gordon and Donn Eric Rosen combined the 2 genera into one. According to the International Rules of Nomenclature, the older name of *Xiphophorus* has precedence over *Platypoecilus*. However, even today, aquarists and scientists still use the common name of platy when discussing species which traditionally fall into that group.

The common name of swordtail has led to a great deal of confusion because, of all the characteristics which separate these 2 groups, the caudal appendage is the least reliable. Some platy species have swordtails and several swordtail species have little or no swordtail.

Throughout this book we have used the species-group concept proposed by Donn E. Rosen in his 1979 paper to define a platy or swordtail, with the additions of those species which have been described since Rosen's paper was published.

Under this scheme the genus *Xiphophorus* is split into 3 species-groups:

- **Group 1** – *andersi*, *couchianus*, *gordoni* and *meyeri*. We have been unable to find a scientific reference already published which places *andersi* in this species-group, or in any other, but Manfred K. Meyer, who was one of the describers of this species, feels that it is most closely allied to this group (personal communication).

- **Group 2** – *evelynae*, *maculatus*, *milleri*, *variatus* and *xiphidium*.

- **Group 3** – *alvarezi*, *birchmanni*, *clemenciae*, *continens*, *cortezi*, *helleri*, *malinche*, *montezumae*, *multilineatus*, *nezahualcoyotl*, *nigrensis*, *pygmaeus* and *signum*.

Group 3 has been further subdivided by Rauchenberger *et al.* (1990) with the 9 swordtails from the Rio Panuco basin being split into 3 clades. These are as follows:

- Cortezi clade – *cortezi*, *birchmanni* and *malinche*.

- Montezumae clade – *montezumae*, *nezahualcoyotl* and *continens*.

- Pygmaeus clade – *pygmaeus*, *nigrensis* and *multilineatus*.

From the aquarists point of view, species-groups 1 and 2 represent what have classically been called platies, whilst species-group 3 represents the swordtails.

1.

3.

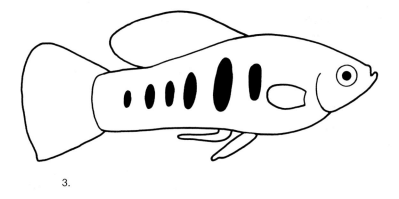

2.

Fig. 2 Vertical bar markings for adult males in the Cortezi clade of *Xiphophorus*. 1. *X. cortezi*. 2. *X. malinche*. 3. *X. birchmanni*.

2
Anatomy

A basic knowledge of the anatomy of *Xiphophorus* and of the features peculiar to the genus is important in understanding how the fish function.

External Covering

Xiphophorus are covered with scales which overlap each other, forming a solid shield. This protects the fish from damage by sharp objects and other fish. The front scale overlaps the scale behind it and so on along the side; this produces a streamlined surface which cuts down on friction. The scales are covered with a mucus coat which helps the fish slip through the water more easily and also protects it against parasitic infestation.

Lateral Line

Running along both sides of the fish from just behind the operculum to the caudal peduncle is the lateral line. This is not always a straight line but will vary from species to species. This line is in fact a sensory organ which consists of a canal in the epidermis containing many smaller sensory organs. These organs are sensitive to sound waves and vibrations, so helping in the detection of other fish and of predators.

Operculum

The hard plate which protects the delicate tissues of the gills is called the operculum. It is hinged at the front and open at the rear to allow the passage of water away from the gills.

Fins

Xiphophorus have 7 fins, of which 3 are unpaired. The dorsal fin acts as a stabilizer and helps the fish stay upright in the water. This fin is usually kept in an upright position. When the fish is unhealthy or unhappy the dorsal will be clamped to the body.

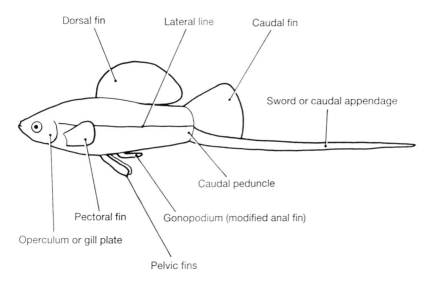

Dorsal fin

Lateral line

Caudal fin

Sword or caudal appendage

Caudal peduncle

Pectoral fin

Gonopodium (modified anal fin)

Operculum or gill plate

Pelvic fins

Fig. 3 Physical features of a male swordtail (*Xiphophorus montezumae*).

The caudal fin is used for propulsion. By curving its body when swimming, the fish cuts down on back pressure, thus increasing the effectiveness of the fin's movement. As a method of propulsion, the caudal fin is so powerful that it can not only move the fish through the water at tremendous speed, but also push the fish right out of the water should it become frightened. For this reason a tight-fitting lid on the aquarium is advisable.

The third unpaired fin is the anal fin. In the female this acts, to a certain degree, as a stabilizer but its small size rather limits its effectiveness in this role. It is in the male *Xiphophorus* that this fin is of vital importance for, as the fish reaches sexual maturity, the anal fin changes shape and forms the gonopodium. This structure is normally carried pointing backwards but it is capable of moving to the right or left until it points forwards.

The pelvic fins are sometimes referred to as the ventral fins. This term, however, is more correctly used for all the fins on the ventral surface of the fish. The pelvic fins once again have a stabilizing function and act in a similar way to the anti-roll devices used by some ships. An absence of 1 of these fins completely upsets the balance of the unfortunate animal.

The pectoral fins are positioned just behind the operculum. These are mainly used to propel the fish forwards, backwards, up and down. They also play an important part in steering and balance.

The sword or caudal appendage is used purely for show when the fish is courting. In fast-flowing water, however, where many of the long-sworded species occur, it may act in a similar fashion to the rudder of a ship.

Gonopodium

Male *Xiphophorus* possess a gonopodium whose structure is unique to each species. At its tip there are a series of barbs and spines which are used by ichthyologists for identification purposes. In the early days of ichthyology the significance of this structure was not realized and a number of species were described from females rather than males. These barbs and spines are used by the fish to hold the male in place during mating. They are often referred to as *holdfasts*. Most species which live in fast-flowing streams have rather large holdfasts, whilst those from sluggish or still waters generally have smaller holdfasts.

The gonopodium is often described as being rod-like, or as a tube – with the inference that it is hollow. In fact the rays of the gonopodium, when relaxed, lie one above the other. When the gonopodium is swung either right or left, the rays fold over and form a groove down which the sperm packets (spermatozeugmata) are channelled towards the vent of the female.

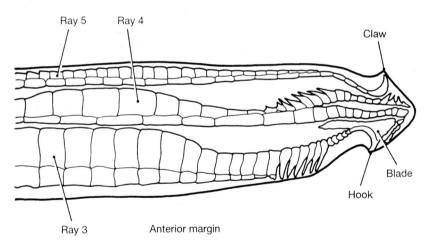

Fig. 4 The gonopodium of a *Xiphophorus helleri*.

3
The Natural Environment

Nearly all the described species of *Xiphophorus* have their centre of distribution in Mexico. This is a country of vast complexity with many different climatic zones. Because it is on the northern edge of the tropical zone, with the Tropic of Cancer passing through the middle of the country, altitude as well as latitude plays an important role in the climate. Throughout Mexico rainfall is generally much greater in the summer than in the winter and reaches its maximum in July, August and September. This means most rivers are faster-flowing and deeper at this time of the year.

Temperatures during the summer are also somewhat higher, although they are greatly affected by the altitude. In the lowland coastal regions, which experience the moderating influence of the sea, the temperature variations between night and day and between summer and winter are much less. This zone is called the Hot Zone or, in Mexico, the Tierra Caliente. It extends up to an altitude of 800 m, which is the highest point at which Cacao can be successfully grown and which is the region where tropical rainforests occur in Mexico. Most platies come from this zone and therefore prefer warmer temperatures than many of the swordtails. An exception to this is species-group 1 – the northern platies. In the area of Mexico where these are found the temperature in January averages 12°C but may fall as low as −5°C. However, these platies usually live in spring-fed pools, where more stable, warmer conditions persist, even when the air temperature drops to dangerously low levels.

Above this zone is the Temperate Zone, which extends from 800 m to 1,700 m. This zone is suitable for the cultivation of such crops as coffee, cotton and sugar-cane. Here the temperature fluctuates much more from season to season and from night to day. Many of the swordtails come from this zone, often being found at elevations above 1,000 m. The Sheepshead Swordtail (*X. birchmanni*), Cortes Swordtail (*X. cortezi*) and the Highland Swordtail (*X. malinche*) have all regularly been caught at temperatures as low as 13°C. The Pueblo Platy (*X. evelynae*) occurs at elevations above 1,000 m and may very well be subjected to cooler temperatures in the wild than its lowland cousins.

One of the major problems for Mexico and its native flora and fauna is the pressure it is under from the human population. In 1910 this was estimated as being 15 million. In 1986 the figure was thought to be over

80 million, with estimates that this would rise to over 120 million by the year 2000. This dramatic increase in population is causing severe financial and ecological problems for Mexico and many other developing countries.

Water is of vital importance to many industries and agriculture, as well as to the population as a whole. To satisfy these needs, water is being drawn from a variety of natural habitats at unsustainable levels. In the Huasteca Canyon, near the city of Monterrey, a number of springs which used to flow year round have dried up. This has led to the near extinction of the Monterrey Platy (*X. couchianus*). In part, this decline is probably only a continuation of a process which has been going on for a long period of time. The 3 most northerly species of *Xiphophorus* (*couchianus*, *gordoni* and *meyeri*) seem to have evolved from a single ancestor which had a widespread range throughout this part of Mexico. Due to increased aridity, and probably a drop in temperature as well, the 3 populations became isolated from each other and evolved into new species. The Apodaca population of *X. couchianus* is still undergoing this process and may well have differentiated enough to be described as a separate species.

Stream flowing under 'Puente Chinoluiz'. This is one of the new locations for *Xiphophorus clemenciae*. *X. helleri* also occurs here. During the rainy season this river will become a veritable flood.

The genus *Xiphophorus* is naturally-occurring in freshwater streams on the Atlantic slopes of Mexico, Guatemala, Belize and Honduras. The platies, in general, prefer to live in habitats with dense aquatic vegetation close to the banks of springs, pools, backwaters and weed-filled ditches. They are usually prolific in such habitats and present little problem when being caught in the wild.

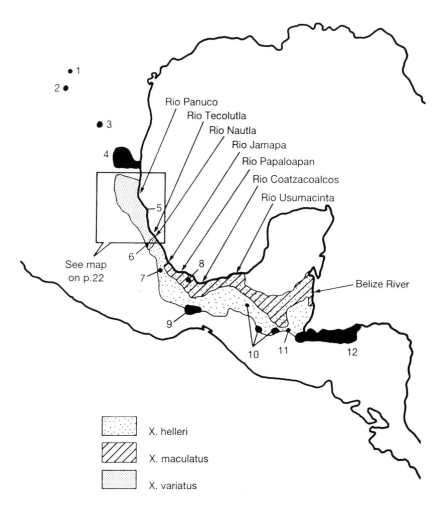

Distribution of *Xiphophorus* species (except Rio Panuco swordtails).
1. *X. meyeri.* 2. *X. gordoni.* 3. *X. couchianus.* 4. *X. xiphidium.*
5. *X. variatus.* 6. *X. evelynae.* 7. *X. andersi.* 8 *X. milleri.*
9. *X. clemenciae.* 10. *X. alvarezi.* 11. *X. signum.* 12. *X.* 'PMH'.

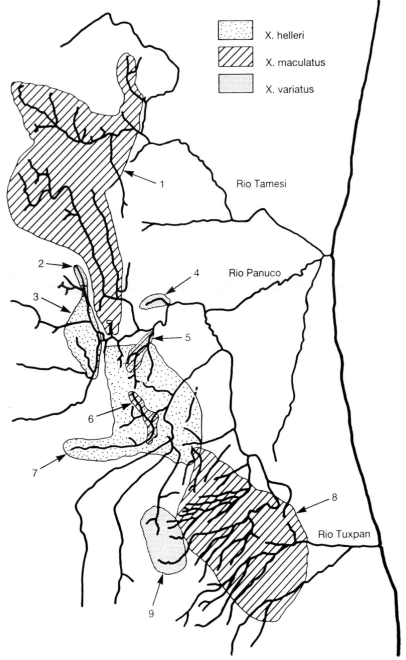

Distribution of Rio Panuco swordtails. 1. *Xiphophorus nezahualcoyotl*.
2. *X. continens*. 3. *X. montezumae*. 4. *X. nigrensis*. 5. *X. multilineatus*.
6. *X. pygmaeus*. 7. *X. cortezi*. 8. *X. birchmanni*. 9. *X. malinche*.

The swordtails, in general, prefer fast-moving water with open areas to swim in. Only gravid females and fry live in the aquatic vegetation near the banks of such habitats. However, the genus *Xiphophorus* is nothing if not adaptable and will be found in a wide range of habitats, from very fast-flowing rivers with little or no plant cover to slow-moving streams with an abundance of plant life. A number of species occur in springs and ponds with little or no water movement and heavy plant growth, whilst others can be found in large lakes with little plant growth except around the edges.

An example of a typical spring habitat is the *nacimiento* (headwater spring) of the Rio Ojo Frio, near the village of El Quince. This is north of the town of Rascon and forms one of the headwaters of the Rio Gallinas in the Rio Panuco system. The springs are tucked away in amongst the trees and, with their steep banks and mud and rock bottoms, are quite difficult to reach.

In general, the adult Montezuma Swordtails (*X. montezumae*) live in the open areas and can be clearly seen in the crystal-clear water. Normally, the adults will feed on insects which fall onto the surface of the water, water insects and, occasionally, on algae which grow on the rocks.

Nacimiento of the Rio Ojo Frio near the village of El Quince. This is a typical spring habitat.

The gravid females move away from the open water into areas of dense plant growth to have their fry. This gives the babies the best chance of survival. The other swordtail species which lives in this habitat is the diminutive El Quince Swordtail (*X. continens*). This species makes the areas of heavy plant growth its home all the time and generally feeds on the insects which thrive amongst the plants and some vegetable matter. The water quality at this location in February 1992 was pH 7.8 and 250 p.p.m. (total hardness).

A fast-flowing river habitat with little plant life is the headwaters of the Rio Choy. This too forms part of the Rio Panuco drainage and is home to the rare El Abra Pygmy Swordtail (*X. nigrensis*). This species only occurs in this one river and, in general, is found most abundantly at the river's outflow from a cave. At this point the river is extremely fast-flowing and the banks are very steep. Once again the adults can be seen in the mid-water regions, fighting against the current. The gravid females move into the sparsely-planted areas to have their babies and these areas form a natural haven for the growing fry. As they become larger and stronger, they migrate out into the main river itself. One peculiarity of this species is the differing size of the males. The large-morph males generally stay in the main part of the river, whilst the small males can be found near the banks. In February 1992 the water quality was found to be of pH 7.6 and 425 p.p.m. (total hardness).

The headwaters of the Rio Choy. The river can be seen flowing out of the cave mouth. *Xiphophorus nigrensis* occurs only in this river.

A beautiful lake with several endemic *Xiphophorus* species is Lake Catemaco. The lake is 16 km long and has an area of 130 km². It is surrounded by volcanic hills and is home to a number of unique species of fish. In the shallow areas of the lake, Green Swordtails (*X. helleri*) are abundant. Once again, to have their babies, the females move into the planted areas which act as nurseries for this species. The Catemaco Platy (*X. milleri*) also lives in these areas of heavy plant growth, probably filling the same niche here as the El Quince Swordtail (*X. continens*) does in the headwaters of the Rio Gallinas. The Green Swordtails and the Catemaco Platies can be found in every inlet to the lake, with many different colour morphs occurring in the numerous habitats.

A typical river habitat, with plenty of plant growth, is the Rio Michol near Palenque, in the state of Chiapas. Here, the Upland Swordtail (*X. alvarezi*) and the Green Swordtail are said to occur together. However, both have similar body forms, colour and finnage, which makes identification very difficult. The identification of the Upland Swordtail from this location is now considered doubtful. In the wild, it appears that both species occupy similar habitats and possible hybrids between the 2 have been found in nature. This is quite rare amongst wild *Xiphophorus*, which normally have a number of isolating mechanisms to prevent this kind of intermingling of species.

As can be seen from just these 4 habitats, platies and swordtails have adapted to a wide range of conditions in the wild. It is this adaptability which has allowed both the man-made and the wild species of platy and swordtail, through the agency of Man, to become established throughout the world, wherever a suitable climate and habitat can be found.

The Green Swordtail and its hybrids have been introduced and established in Florida, Wyoming and Arizona, in thermal outflows in Idaho, Canada and the UK (these populations may not survive in the long term), and in Nevada, California, Hawaii, Puerto Rico, Fiji, Gaum, South Africa, Sri Lanka and Australia. The Australian populations are centred on Brisbane, but further populations have now been found in Queensland. In geothermally-heated swamps at the southern edge of Lake Taupo in New Zealand, a population of Green Swordtails has recently become established. At the moment, this seems to be centred on Waipahihi stream, where the water has a temperature range of 22–48°C (Vincent & Forsyth, 1987). Within Mexico itself, Contreras and Escalante (1984) reported that introductions of this species have occurred in Michoacán, Morelos, Nuevo León and Coalhuila. In 1990 I found various introduced populations of the Green Swordtail in the state of Jalisco, Mexico. All these introductions are thought to be releases of unwanted pet fish or, very occasionally, intentional releases for mosquito control.

The Variable Platy (*X. variatus*) has been introduced to Florida,

Lake Catemaco. This is a beautiful lake teaming with aquatic life. *Xiphophorus milleri* and *X. helleri* occur together here.

Rio Michol near Palenque. This is a typical river habitat with plenty of plant growth. *Xiphophorus helleri* lives here together with *X. maculatus* and a number of other livebearers.

California, Hawaii, Montana (in thermal springs), Arizona and Columbia. All of these appear to be descendants of pet fish which have been dumped in local rivers. The Southern Platy (*X. maculatus*) has been introduced into Nevada, Florida, California, Texas, Hawaii, Puerto Rico, Nigeria, Saudi Arabia, Palau and Columbia. Australia has several well-established populations of this species. These can be found in the small creeks and swamps to the north of Brisbane, in the upper Brisbane River and in Hervey Bay. In Mexico, Contreras and Escalante (1984) have reported populations becoming established in springs in Coahuila, Guanajuato, Nuevo León and Sonora. A population had already become established in the Rio Teuchitlan, Jalisco, and may have been at least partly responsible for the possible extinction of the livebearing Golden Sawfin goodeid (*Skiffia francesae*). Apparently, in the mid-1970s, the introduced fish were Red Platies but, by the time I visited this location in 1990, they had reverted into nondescript grey fish with a few black markings and a slight bronze sheen. This coloration is very similar to that of many of the wild populations of this species. The adult size of these fish had decreased as well; the largest fish caught was a female only 35 mm long. Once again, these introductions seem to have resulted from an aquarist releasing his surplus stocks directly into the local river. Another possible source might be a shop-keeper releasing fish into the local river so that he could come back at a later date and collect his own fish rather than have to buy them.

   All these introductions have led to the decline of the endemic species. In some cases (such as the Golden Sawfin Goodeid), this has led to the extinction, or near extinction, of some of the native fish. In general, platy and swordtail introductions have only been damaging to the native populations through increased competition, whilst other species of poeciliid, most notably the Western Mosquitofish (*Gambusia affinis*), have caused wholesale damage to the native fauna through predation. This species was even dubbed the 'Fish Destroyer' by Myers in 1965 because of the damage it was doing to the native species in areas where it had been introduced to help control mosquitoes. The irony is that many of these native species were even more efficient at destroying mosquitoes than the Western Mosquitofish and, with the elimination of the native fish, the mosquito population increased.

4

The Aquarium Environment

Platies and swordtails have the reputation of being extremely hardy fish and ideally suited to the beginner because they will survive conditions in which other less adaptable fish will die. Whilst this is partly true for the cultivated forms found in most aquarium shops, it is certainly not the case with the wild forms. Whilst by no means delicate fish, they still require good conditions to thrive and realize their full potential.

Water

Water is a compound of two gases – hydrogen and oxygen – and is one of nature's greatest solvents. It is found in its purest form when just beginning to fall from the clouds but, during its descent to the ground, it absorbs numerous impurities. Once it is on the ground, other substances dissolve into it and, if it is being collected for domestic use, various chemicals will be added to kill bacteria and make the water safe for drinking.

From an aquarist's point of view a number of variables are of importance to the well-being of their fish and these are discussed below.

pH

This is a measurement of how acid or alkaline the water is, the most acidic solution possible being denoted as 0.0 and the strongest alkaline solution as 14.0. Pure distilled water, being neither acid nor alkaline, has a pH value of 7.0.

This value is important to a number of delicate species of fish all the time and to many others when an attempt is being made to breed them. Sudden drastic changes in the pH value can kill fish, so care should be taken when introducing new fish to a tank. There are many good testing-kits on the market which are reasonably accurate and easy to use. There are also a number of chemicals available to adjust the pH value up or down according to your needs.

Hardness

Aquarists very often confuse hardness with pH because soft water tends to be acidic whilst hard water tends to be alkaline. The two values, however, are quite independent. To further add to this confusion, hardness can be measured in a number of different ways. In the UK it is usually measured on Clark's scale where $1° = 14.3$ p.p.m. calcium carbonate. In Germany $1°dH = 17.9$ p.p.m. calcium oxide. To convert from the German to the English system simply multiply by 0.56. Another way to express hardness is in p.p.m. calcium carbonate. Up to 100 p.p.m. $(6°dH)$ is considered soft whilst over 450 p.p.m. $(25°dH)$ is very hard. Once again there are many good test-kits on the market and there are a number of chemicals which can raise or lower the hardness to the level you require.

Additives

Chlorine and other additives in tap water can create a problem if present at high levels in your supply. Water authorities are under no obligation to provide water which is suitable for your fish; they need only supply water which is safe for you to drink. Keep a lookout in your local paper for announcements of when extra chemicals will be added to your supply and never do a water-change if the tap water is cloudy. There are many preparations on the market which will render chlorine harmless to fish. However, if only 20 per cent of the water is changed at any one time, you should not need to use these chemicals. Many fish kills attributed to chlorine are usually due to a drastic change in pH or to some other additive in the tap water.

Salt

This is often considered to be an important additive to an aquarium which contains platies and swordtails. Just how and why this myth began is something of a mystery since wild *Xiphophorus* are very rarely found in anything but pure fresh water. If they are maintained in soft, acidic conditions then a little salt in the water may help to buffer the pH, but, since there are more effective substances on the market now to raise pH to the desired level, it is far better to leave the packet of salt where it belongs – in the kitchen.

Suitable conditions for most *Xiphophorus* species are anywhere between pH 7.2 and pH 8.0 and a hardness of about 15–25° dH. As a generality, swordtails prefer their water harder and more alkaline than platies. This is especially true of many of the Rio Panuco basin swordtails, which come from headwater springs where the water has permeated through limestone and become extremely hard and alkaline. There are some exceptions to this which will be dealt with in Chapter 10.

Maintenance of water quality

In general, swordtails come from clean, fast-flowing water which has a high oxygen content and these species are the first to show signs of stress if the water quality deteriorates. Platies are more often found in slower-moving water or ponds and can tolerate poor water quality and low levels of oxygen better than many other fish. However, just because a fish can survive poor conditions doesn't mean it will thrive in them. Therefore, a good aquarium environment is essential for the well-being of all platies and swordtails, regardless of species.

In an enclosed aquatic ecosystem such as an aquarium there is a delicate balance between a healthy environment and a deadly one. The dissolved waste products of fish, primarily ammonia, are toxic and cause damage to the gills and, in high concentrations, can cause brain damage and death.

Normally ammonia is converted into nitrite by *Nitrosomonas* bacteria which live in the water of all tanks. The *Nitrobacter* which live on all the surfaces of gravel, rocks etc. convert this nitrite into nitrate. These substances are somewhat less poisonous than ammonia but high levels are still harmful to fish and need to be removed.

Balanced-tank System

Under natural conditions, growing plants absorb the nitrate and use it as a food, thereby acting as the filters of the natural world. This cycle needs to be replicated within the aquarium if the ammonia is not to build up to dangerous levels and kill the fish. This can be done in a number of ways but the process in the natural environment can be simulated most closely by creating a balanced aquarium. In such a tank the stocking levels of fish are kept relatively low and plenty of growing plants are added to break down the nitrates and other waste products.

One of the arguments used against such a system is what happens at night. All living things breathe in oxygen and give out carbon dioxide. Carbon dioxide is a poison which can kill fish if the levels become too high. During the day the plants are receiving light and photosynthesising. This process breaks down carbon dioxide into carbohydrates, which the plants use as a food, and oxygen, which they give off from their leaves.

However, at night, the plants can no longer photosynthesise because light is essential to this process, but they continue to breathe, thus adding even more carbon dioxide to the water. Only so much of this gas can escape from the surface of the water and be replaced by oxygen from the atmosphere; therefore, the fish suffer stress and perhaps death due to carbon-dioxide poisoning.

The theory is sound enough as far as it goes, but what is missing is how the fish are behaving at this time. Night-time is a period of rest for most fish. Whilst asleep, they are using far less oxygen than they do during the day so the carbon-dioxide levels never build up to danger point.

Filtration

The advantages of the balanced-tank system are the low set-up costs and the minimal maintenance required. Its one disadvantage is that most aquarists like more fish in their aquarium than this sort of system can comfortably support. For this reason a form of filtration is required. There are 3 types of filtration mechanism.

Chemical The most common chemical filtration medium used in aquaria is activated carbon, which absorbs waste products onto its surface. It is usually sandwiched between layers of filter floss and must be changed on a regular basis to remain effective. Recently a substance called Zeolite, which absorbs ammonia, has come onto the market. This cannot be used when salt has been added to the tank as its absorptive properties are blocked by this substance. To 'recharge' Zeolite, it should be soaked in some salty water overnight and then rinsed thoroughly with fresh water.

Mechanical There are many mechanical filters on the market, ranging from simple plastic boxes, using an air-lift to pull water through a filter floss or sponge, to power-filters which pump the water through a sponge. All of these rely on regular cleaning of the filter medium or they become ineffective.

Biological These rely on the *Nitrobacter* to break down the wastes into the far less harmful nitrates. Under-gravel filters push the water through the gravel bed to provide a very large surface area on which the *Nitrobacter* can live. The gravel bed needs to be at least 5 cm deep for this to be effective and plants will often suffer because of the water movement around their roots. Many power-filters have an element of biological filtration in their action. However, they are only effective if not clogged with mulm and other solids. The foam filter medium must be carefully washed out in water of the same temperature otherwise the bacteria will be killed off and take days to re-establish.

Aeration can significantly increase the number of fish a tank will support. However, if there is a power-cut or the pump fails then the carbon-dioxide level will build up as the oxygen level falls and a crisis point is quickly reached, at which time the fish start to die. It is therefore safer to have only as many fish in the tank as the oxygen absorbed at the surface can support. This can be calculated from the following formula which gives you the number of centimetres of fish a tank can support:

$$\frac{\text{Length in cm} \times \text{Width in cm}}{20}$$

Therefore a tank 60 cm × 30 cm in area can house 90 cm of fish. If the average *adult* size of fish you are keeping is 5 cm then you can safely have 18 fish in the tank.

Water-changes

Another alternative to using filters is to carry out very large, regular, partial water-changes and to keep the number of fish in the tank to the level stated above. Personally, this is the system which we use and all our tanks are subjected to an 80 per cent water-change each week. Some aquarists change as much as 60 per cent every day. What this process does is to remove all the waste products from the aquarium, thus obviating the need for filtration. It also means that the fish can be fed very generously, thus making them grow much more quickly and to a greater size. The disadvantages with this system are the hard work involved and the necessity to keep up with the water-changes. If the tank misses its water-change then the fish can be at serious risk from ammonia poisoning within a week.

Whatever system you opt for, even filtration and aeration will not completely obviate the need to carry out water-changes. A minimum of 20 per cent of the tank water should be changed every week with fresh water of the same temperature.

Heating

The majority of tropical fish are far more adaptable to temperature than we give them credit for. In the wild a pool may be 16°C first thing in the morning but reach 35°C by mid-afternoon. Such wild swings in temperature do not harm the fish in that pool because they have adapted to them over many generations and because the changes occur over a period of hours. A *sudden* change of such a magnitude would more than likely kill the same fish outright.

For platies and swordtails, the ideal temperature to aim for is 21–24°C. Higher temperatures will speed up the metabolism of the fish and shorten their lives, whilst lower temperatures will make them sluggish and cause them to lose their colour.

Heating the aquarium is simplicity itself today, with a good range of reliable combined heater/thermostats on the market. Depending on the size of the tank, different wattage heaters will be required to maintain the temperature comfortably. As a rough guide, allow 10W per 4.5 l of water, e.g. a 45 cm × 25 cm × 25 cm tank which contains 27 l of water will require a 60W heater. If a 60W heater is not available then you must go for the next available wattage up, which, in this case, would most likely be 100W.

Should you suffer a power-cut in winter, or should the heater/thermostat break down, cover the tank with a blanket to keep the heat in. Once the heating is back on, allow the tank to return to its correct temperature slowly. Never pour in hot water to keep the temperature up as this can cause more damage than would a short period at a lower temperature. Make sure you keep an eye on the fish for the next few days in case whitespot develops due to chilling.

Lighting

Adequate lighting is essential for proper plant growth and for you to see the fish. At one time only tungsten bulbs were used to light aquaria but there are now many different kinds of fluorescent tubes available, each with its own distinctive spectrum. These lights enhance the growth of the plants and/or bring out the colours of the fish.

There are no hard and fast rules regarding the amount of light needed above a tank to provide adequate illumination for plant growth, since a great deal will depend on the siting of the tank, how deep it is, and how much daylight it receives. Ideally start with a fluorescent tube which is almost as long as the tank, i.e. a 37.5 cm tube for a 45 cm tank. If, after a period of time, it is clear that the plants are dying rather than growing, but no algae are forming, then you will need to add another tube to the tank. If there is rampant algal growth, then add more plants and shade the tank from direct sunlight. If algae are still a problem after the plants have become established, then you will need to reduce the wattage of the light or provide more shade at the surface of the tank. A floating plant, such as duckweed, provides good shade and will thrive in many aquaria.

Plants in the Aquarium

There are a tremendous variety of plants on the market. However, many of these are not truly aquatic but are in fact marginals, or even house-plants which will die off during the course of several weeks. Since the tank will have a pH on the alkaline side, plants which suit this environment should be selected in preference to those which like acidic

conditions. Other important factors to consider are the eventual height
that the plants will achieve and the differing coloration and leaf types
available.

Recommended Plants

Anubias nana   The leaves of this small slow-growing species only
achieve 7–10 cm in height. The rhizome grows horizontally along the
bottom of the aquarium and can be divided to make more plants. It
prefers a rich substrate and moderate light and is a very slow grower,
ideal for the foreground of the aquarium.

Aponogeton undulatum   This species and its relatives are tall plants
which reach upwards of 40 cm in height. The tuberous rootstock or bulb
is often sold without any leaves growing from it and should be planted
with the growing tip just above the substrate. The leaves will usually
sprout within a few weeks. They like bright light and, when established,
will send flower spikes above the water. The pale mauve flowers will
produce pollen which can be distributed with a soft brush so that the
seeds will develop.

Bacopa caroliniana   A tall slow-growing plant, *B. carolina* should be
planted in clumps of 3 to 6 stems. These slowly root themselves and new
growth takes place both at the top of the stem and from side-shoots.
When the stem reaches the top of the water, it can be cut in half and the
top portion used to make new clumps. It is not an easy plant to establish
because it requires good lighting and careful handling but the bright,
light green foliage and small, neat, rounded leaves make an attractive
addition to the aquarium.

Cryptocoryne spp.   This very diverse group includes many marginal
species and a great many true aquatics. They vary in height from 5 cm to
50 cm and have bright green through to red leaves. Suitable tall species
are *affinis*, *blassi*, *bulbosus*, *ciliata*, *griffithii* and *harteliana*. Small
species include *beckettii*, *nevillii*, *pontederifolia*, *willisii* and *wendtii*. All
reproduce by runners and most can tolerate low levels of illumination.
When a plant is moved to a new tank, the leaves may die back very
quickly but, provided the roots are undamaged, it will regenerate itself
fairly quickly. This group is one of the most useful of small foreground
plants and also red-foliage plants.

Echinodoras spp.   Another diverse group, this contains many suitable
plants for the *Xiphophorus* tank. Smallest of these is the Pygmy Chain
Sword. This reaches only about 5 cm in height and makes a wonderful
plant for the front of the aquarium. The Amazon Sword plant grows up

to 50 cm in height and has bright green, sword-shaped leaves. In good condition, it is a marvellous specimen plant. Propagation is by runners which develop many plantlets along its length. These can be cut off when they have developed roots and are large enough.

Marsilia quadrifolia   Also known as Four-Leaf Clover, this makes an interesting addition to the foreground of the aquarium. It only achieves a height of some 7–10 cm and its stems terminate in a flat leaf which looks somewhat like a Clover leaf. It is difficult to establish and prefers a fine substrate.

Hygrophila polysperma   A firm favourite in the aquarium hobby since it was first introduced in the 1940s, this is a tall plant whose single stems are best planted in clumps of 3 to 6 at the back of the aquarium. They soon grow up to the top and send out side-shoots. Reproduction is by cuttings which can be taken every week once the plant is established.

Limnophila sessiliflora (Ambulia)   This is a feathery-leaved plant, ideal for the rear of the aquarium, but it requires strong light and a lime-free substrate. It should be planted in bunches and is propagated by cuttings.

Myriophyllum   Also known as Parrot's Feather, this is by far and away the best of the feathery-leaved plants. It requires good lighting but does well in alkaline water and establishes more easily than many plants of this type. Plant it in clumps of 3 to 6 stems from which cuttings can be taken once they have grown to the surface of the water.

Sagittaria natans   Excellent aquarium plants, *S. natans* and its relatives will grow in almost any conditions. Most species reach 20 cm or more in height so are best used at the rear and sides of the tank. Propagation is by runners which will form a dense thicket in a comparatively short time.

Vallisneria torta   This species and its relatives are another group of excellent aquarium plants. The leaves grow up to 50 cm long and trail across the surface of the water. They do well in most conditions but extremes of light (too bright or too dim) should be avoided. Reproduction is by means of runners. These will form a dense thicket which will gradually expand and fill the tank if allowed to.

Lay-out

At its most basic, the platy or swordtail tank needs nothing more than clean water of the correct temperature for the fish to survive. For breeding purposes, a clump of Java Moss on the bottom will provide cover for new-born fry or females which are being harassed by over-amorous males. However, from an aesthetic point of view, a properly-furnished tank with a group of beautiful platies or swordtails on show makes a lovely sight.

A group of rocks placed towards one side of the aquarium near the back will provide some height and extra places for the fish to hide. Bogwood, whilst looking very attractive, will leach acids into the water, thus lowering the pH, which may cause problems with these alkaline-water fish. Therefore, it is wise to avoid real bogwood and use one of the artificial alternatives instead. If you do include some rocks, make sure they are safe for use in an aquarium. If in doubt, it is best to purchase these from an aquarium shop.

The plants should be placed around the back and sides of the tank, with the tallest species towards the rear. Generally clumps of the same kind look better than long rows or odd stems of various plants. Low-growing types should be planted in front of the rocks to give these a more natural look.

An alternative to a natural-looking tank is one in which coloured gravel is used on the base. Black produces quite a stunning effect when combined with white rocks, green plants and red swordtails or platies. Using red gravel and black fish can work just as well.

5
Stocking the Aquarium

When buying platies and swordtails there are certain things to look for which will give you the best chance of establishing the new fish in your set-up.

Purchasing Stock

Whether you buy a common Red Platy from your local aquarium shop or a pair of the newest and rarest swordtails from a private breeder, the rules are pretty much the same.

Choosing an Aquarium Shop

Not all aquarium shops offer either the same standard of service or quality of fish. Here are some questions which you need to ask yourself when visiting an aquarium shop.

- Are all the tanks clean and well maintained?
- Are all the fish healthy?
- Is sound advice being offered to customers?

If the answer is 'yes' to all these questions then take a closer look at the fish to see if there is anything you want to buy.

Choosing a Private Breeder

Similarly not all private breeders offer either the same standard of service or quality of fish. If you are buying cultivated fish you will want to know the genetic background of the strain and how long the breeder has been working with it. With wild species you must be even more choosy and insist on being supplied with collection data – where and when the strain was collected – and the name of the original supplier.

One problem which is of particular importance with wild fish is hybridization. This is where 2 species have interbred and the fish are no longer the true species. Many *Xiphophorus* species will freely hybridize in the aquarium if 2 or more species are maintained together. It has been suggested that if both sexes of both species are present in the tank then each species will breed only with its own kind. Unfortunately, this is just not the case because the normal isolating mechanisms which work in the wild fail in the confines of an aquarium. Therefore, when looking round a private breeder's set-up, check to make sure only 1 species of *Xiphophorus* is maintained in each tank. Hybrids and misidentified fish are, unfortunately, quite common in the hobby, so a little care in selecting who you buy your fish from can save you a lot of heartache in the future.

Selecting Stock

Once you have decided what you want to buy, have a close look at all the fish in the tank to determine which ones you want. Choose those which have their fins spread and are swimming around the tank looking happy. Avoid fish which have their fins clamped or are shimmying (this is a slow side-to-side motion) as these are both signs of illness. Look for fish with a good robust body shape; thin or wasted fish should be avoided as these may be seriously ill. Once you have made your selections make sure the shop-keeper or breeder catches the particular fish you want. Never be prepared to take whatever they catch for you as the best will often be held back.

Transporting Fish

Once you have bought your new fish you should take it home as soon as possible. Make sure you keep it at a safe temperature. This does not have to be exactly that of the aquarium but extremes must be avoided. Never leave fish in the boot of your car or in the back window on a hot day because you could end up with poached platy for tea that night! Ideally, obtain a polystyrene box from your local aquarium shop so that, when you go on a fish-hunting expedition, you have something to put your purchases in.

If you have travelled overseas to obtain fish, then you could be on the road for several days or even longer. Provided that the fish are packed properly this should not prove too much of a problem. Each individual fish needs to be bagged separately in a large bag with clean water. Check all the fish every morning and evening and, if the water is looking cloudy, it should be filtered through a paper towel or filter floss.

If you are travelling in an aircraft then you may have problems taking fish into the cabin as, technically speaking, they are animals. To be safe, it is best to take with you a small polystyrene box, which will fit inside your suitcase, to house any fish. In this way you will not be breaking any regulations and the fish will be kept warm throughout the journey. You must also have an import licence as it is illegal to bring fish into many countries without one.

Introducing New Fish to the Aquarium

All new purchases should be quarantined in an isolation tank for at least 2 weeks before introducing them to your community tank. The isolation tank should be left bare except for a small box-filter with filter floss and some rocks or plastic plants for cover. Check the fish every day to make sure they are looking healthy and happy. All equipment for this tank should *only* be used in the isolation tank and you must make sure your wash your hands after working in it.

If you are using levamisole as a prophylactic treatment (to prevent parasitic worms from being introduced into your set-up), you should treat the newly-purchased fish when they first go into the quarantine tank. The dosage should then be repeated the day before the fish are moved into their permanent home.

When introducing new fish to an aquarium, the tank lights need to be turned off and the fish in the main tank fed. Open the bag containing the new fish and float it at the surface for half an hour to allow the temperatures to equalize. Check the pH values of the water in both your tank and the bag to make sure they are similar. If there is more than 0.5 of a unit difference then add the tank water to the bag over a period of several hours so that the fish gradually become adjusted to the new conditions.

Over the next few days, carefully watch your new additions to make sure they have not suffered from the change in conditions and are not being bullied by the other fish in the tank. Sometimes problems will occur between 2 fish which can only be resolved by the removal of one or other of the protagonists.

6
Diet

Your fish's diet is of greatest importance to their well-being as only a balanced diet will produce healthy fish.

Essential Constituents of Foods

All foods contain 5 main components, all of which must be present to produce a well-balanced diet.

Proteins

These are the building blocks of the body. They replace worn-out tissues and build new ones as growth proceeds. Good sources of protein are meat, eggs, cheese and beans.

Carbohydrates

Energy is produced from these foods. Good sources are sugar and cereals.

Fats

These are used as a reserve supply of food and help to produce energy and nourish the nervous system.

Minerals

These include a wide spectrum of substances, such as calcium and iron which are essential for healthy teeth and bones and for the proper functioning of the circulatory and nervous systems. They are present in most foods.

Vitamins

In recent years, the role vitamins play in promoting good health and preventing disease has become more widely known. Many human beings now take multi-vitamin supplements for their own health. Good natural sources for these are fresh fruits and vegetables.

Types of Fish-foods

The great variety of prepared and live foods for fish falls into 4 basic categories.

Dried Foods

A vast number of dried foods are available on the market today and, whilst most of them are a complete food in themselves, it is wise to give your fish a feeding of live food at least once a week. If you want to achieve good growth rates with your fry, then high-protein foods will have to be fed.

Fresh, Tinned or Frozen Foods

Just about anything which you eat yourself can be fed to your fish. Good foods to try are: any lean meat chopped finely, cheese, hard-boiled eggs, crab, fish roe and any cooked vegetable.

With the advent of the food-blender, home-produced fish-foods became easy to prepare. If you place any or all of the above-mentioned items in a blender with a little hot water and gelatine you will produce a thick paste which will set. This should then be spooned into ice-cube trays and frozen. A cube can then be thawed out before being fed to the fish.

Live Foods

Whatever species of fish you are working with, all seem to do better if live foods are included in their diet. There is a wide variety available to the aquarist and these may either be purchased from the local aquarium shop or cultured at home.

Various small worms have been cultured by aquarists for many years and, whilst they require a little fuss and bother, they are still an extremely cheap and good source of food for your fish.

Microworms (*Anguillila silusiae*) These are the smallest of the worms and are ideal for new-born fish. To culture these worms all you need is a few old margarine tubs with a small hole pierced in the lids and some porridge. The porridge should be mixed with water until it becomes a thick paste and then spooned into the tubs until it forms a layer about 2.5 cm thick on the bottom. A small spoonful of starter culture is placed on top and the lid put on. After about 2 days, tiny white worms will be seen on the sides of the tub. These can be wiped off and fed to the fish. Because the cultures go off after about 4–6 days, fresh cultures should be started every few days to keep a constant supply.

Grindal Worms The next size up are the Grindal Worms. These measure up to 5 mm long and need different treatment from Micro-worms. The culture medium should be a peat-type compost. Ideally, one of the artificial peat-substitutes should be used. The compost needs to be well moistened and a small depression should be made in the middle. The starter culture should be placed in this and a spoonful of porridge paste put on top. A small piece of glass is then used to cover the depression and the lid put on. The culture should be kept at a temperature of about 24°C and, within a week, there will be enough worms to feed to your fish. Add a little more food as the worms eat it and start new cultures on a monthly basis.

Whiteworms (*Enchytraeus albidus*) These are the largest of the more commonly cultured worms and reach a length of about 4 cm. These are cultured in the same way as Grindal Worms except that they prefer a temperature of 10–15°C.

Mosquito Larvae Another good food, these can be cultured in just about any vessel which holds water. Stand the container outside, filled with water, and add some old leaves or potato peelings to start an infusoria culture. The smell given off by the stagnant water will attract mosquitoes to lay their eggs in it. These then hatch out into little larvae which can be fed to your fish. The only drawback to this food is that the female mosquitoes may take a bite out of you to provide the nourishment they need to lay eggs!

Brine Shrimp (*Artemia sp.*) By far and away the best live food available is Brine Shrimps. These can be purchased as adults from aquarium shops or babies can be hatched from the dried eggs. The former are excellent for adult fish and the latter are probably the best food available for baby fish. There are many different brands of Brine-shrimp egg on the market now. Not all have a good hatch rate and some come from polluted sources and may be detrimental to the fish. When selecting a brand, choose one which has batch numbers and an analysis of hatch rate and pollutants. It may cost more but you can be sure of the results. Hatching instructions are usually given on the container.

Pond Foods

There is a wide spectrum of animals living in ponds which make excellent additions to your fish's diet. Best known are *Daphnia*,

Bloodworms, Glassworms, *Cyclops* and *Tubifex* worms. There is a small risk of introducing parasites to your aquarium with these foods. However, since they are often in a feast-or-famine situation in the wild, it makes good sense to freeze them down for future use. In this way, any parasites collected with them are killed off and you will have an excellent food for months to come.

7

Diseases

Whilst there are many diseases which afflict tropical fish, their effects can be minimalized if all new fish are carefully selected and properly quarantined and a healthy environment maintained in the aquarium. However, no matter how careful you are, diseases will crop up from time to time and a good book on the subject should form a part of every aquarist's library. Of the more commonly-seen diseases the following, with notes on diagnosis and treatment, are most often associated with *Xiphophorus*.

Whitespot *Ichthyophthirius multifiliis*

This is dealt with first because it is by far and away the commonest disease seen in tropical fish. The symptoms are quite distinctive: clamped fins, flicking and small white spots over much of the body and fins. There are many commercial preparations on the market which are effective against this parasite but early diagnosis and treatment will help prevent losses. Treat the whole tank for this disease.

Velvet Disease *Oodinium limneticum*

This is not so common as whitespot but has many of the same symptoms: clamped fins, flicking and very tiny yellowish spots over the body and fins. Youngsters of many fish are particularly prone to this parasite. Once again there are many effective commercial preparations on the market. The whole tank will need treatment for this disease.

Parasitic Worms *Camallanus* spp.

These were once a relatively small problem within the aquarium hobby but, in recent years, cases of parasitic-worm infestations have grown. Symptoms are as follows: loss of appetite, listlessness, shimmying, poor colour, loss of weight and, in some *but not all cases*, small brownish worms hanging from the vent of the fish. These worms are livebearing and, once in a tank, will slowly infect all the fish. Since only fish heavily infested with worms show any symptoms, it is very easy for this parasite to spread to all the inhabitants of an aquarium before it is noticed. The most effective treatment is only available from your veterinary surgeon and is normally used to treat cattle and sheep for worms. The active ingredient is levamisole and the different brands come at 2.5, 5 and 7.5 per cent strength. The dosage will vary according to the strength of the solution you obtain but, for the 7.5 per cent solution, dosage is 1 ml to 75 l of aquarium water. Ideally, this treatment should be used as a prophylactic on all fish when they are in quarantine.

Tuberculosis *Mycobacterium* spp.

In this disease, infected fish continue to feed normally but still lose weight. Damage to the internal organs of the fish occurs and ulcers can break out anywhere on the body.

Generally, treatment is very difficult and few fish showing positive symptoms of this disease respond to treatment. Antibiotic treatment of the other fish in the tank will usually prevent any further losses but caution is needed once this disease has been diagnosed as it is one of the very few fish diseases which can be caught by human beings. In human beings it usually takes the form of infected nodules on the skin.

Shimmying

Whilst not a disease in itself, many platies and swordtails show this symptom when they are unhappy with the water conditions. It is characterized by a slow weaving motion whilst the fish remains stationary in the water and is often accompanied by loss of appetite and poor colour. High levels of ammonia, nitrate or nitrite can bring it on, as can too much salt in the water. Whatever the cause, a large water-change may 'cure' the affected fish in a matter of hours.

8
Breeding

Livebearers such as *Xiphophorus* have the reputation of being very easy to breed. This is simply because they are usually the first of any aquarist's fish to produce babies. However, whilst obtaining some fry from a cultivated fish bought in a local aquarium shop should not be too difficult, producing a good-quality cultivated strain of livebearer requires many years of dedicated hard work.

The wild forms of platies and swordtails are, in general, much harder to breed than the cultivated varieties. They require good aquarium conditions and a top-quality diet to be at their best. Even when everything is perfect for them, broods usually only number some 10–40 and occur once a month. When compared to most of the egg-layers, which may produce several hundred eggs at every spawning, and which spawn as often as 4 times a month, you can see just how much more fecund egg-layers can be than livebearers.

Sexing Fish

In females and immature males the anal fin is composed of approximately 9 rays bound together by connective tissue. When the fish is healthy and happy, this fin will be held spread out like a fan. However, as the males reach sexual maturity, rays 3, 4 and 5 thicken and elongate to form the gonopodium. At its tip there are a number of bones which form hooks and with which the male secures himself to the female during mating.

Much has been said in hobby literature about sex changes occurring amongst *Xiphophorus*. (This is where a fully-functioning female changes sex and becomes a fully-functional male.) Just how often, if ever, this really occurs is not known. In all the cases which I have investigated, no female fish which gave birth has ever proven to then become a male which fathered fry. The majority of these cases turned out to be exceptional males which took much longer to sex out than their brothers. Occasionally, some were females which developed secondary male characteristics with old age. However, they did not become fully-functional males or even attempt to mate with females.

Every so often a species of *Xiphophorus* will produce a sex ratio other than 1 male to 1 female. In some cases almost 100 per cent male or female broods have been reported. Whilst environmental factors such as pH and temperature have been known to produce skewed sex ratios in other poeciliids, most cases in the *Xiphophorus* genus seem to be linked to the sex chromosomes of the strains concerned. Many wild strains of Green Swordtail regularly produce skewed sex ratios, even in the wild. This has led some scientists to suggest that *X. helleri* does not have sex chromosomes but this is by no means proven at this time. Another factor which is known to affect sex ratios is the size and age at which the father sexed out. Small, early-maturing males often produce broods with a predominance of males, whilst the late-maturing males produce female-biased broods.

When working with cultivated fish, this problem is intensified by certain populations of the Southern Platy (*X. maculatus*) having 3 sex chromosomes (W, X and Y) instead of the usual 2 chromosomes. Since just about every cultivated platy or swordtail will have *X. maculatus* blood in its ancestry somewhere, skewed sex ratios, particularly after a new outcross, often occur and may cause major problems.

Breeding Biology

During mating, the male swings his gonopodium forwards and attaches himself to the female's vent by means of the hook and claw. Removal of one of these holdfasts reduces the likelihood of successful mating, whilst removal of both will prevent it altogether. In strains of cultivated swordtail or platy in which the anal fin is elongated, e.g. Lyretails, males are unable to mate because the holdfasts are only poorly formed and the male is unable to adjust to the fin's greater length. Cutting the gonopodium down to the correct length will enable the male to position it correctly but successfull mating will still not be achieved, as the cut-down gonopodium will still not have the necessary holdfasts.

Once the male is in the correct position, sperm bundles, or spermozeugmata, are released which travel down a groove in the gonopodium and into the female's urogenital aperture. This all takes place in 1–4 seconds. Once the spermozeugmata enter the female, they start to break up and release thousands of sperm. These migrate to the folds lining the ovary and gonoduct and live there until the next batch of eggs is ready for fertilization. Sperm is fed whilst being stored by the female and may live many months until an egg becomes available for fertilization. In general, if another male comes along and mates with her before the next batch of eggs is ready for fertilization, then it will be the newer sperm which will have precedence. However, mixed broods are most often produced.

Gestation takes 20–30 days, depending on temperature. After the first 4 or 5 days, however, the embryo is almost completely formed, with the rest of the gestation time being taken up with the development of the organs. When the babies are ready to be born, the ovarian walls start to contract and the embryo is pushed into the ovarian cavity, down the gonoduct and out into the world. At this stage, the yolk sac may be completely absorbed, but in the majority of cases there is still some left. This will be absorbed in the 12 hours after birth.

Feeding Breeding-stock

With livebearers, even more than egg-layers, a good diet when the fish is breeding is absolutely essential. The female provides some nutriment for the developing embryos and, if the diet is poor, the young produced will often not be as good as they could have been. The female will also suffer, as she will have had to use some of her stored reserves, and may take longer to recover than she might otherwise have done. The next brood may be badly affected as well, with both size and quality of fry being poor. It is a classic case of only getting out what you put in.

Therefore, it is wise to increase the amount of live food in your fish's diet when they are breeding. The new-born young will do better and reach a greater final size if they are fed on foods which are rich in protein. For this reason, live baby Brine Shrimps should constitute a large proportion of the diet during the babies' first few weeks of life. If growth is poor at this stage then the fish never seem to make it up in later life and always remain small and stunted.

The Natural Colony

Breeding *Xiphophorus* species can be effected in either of 2 ways. The commonest is to isolate a female to save the fry, and then to rear these by themselves. When working with the cultivated forms, this selective breeding is essential to maintain or improve the strain. However, with the wild forms, it is possible to flock-breed a species. This eliminates the need for separate fry tanks and, provided that it is done properly, the colony will maintain itself for many years.

The first step in establishing a natural colony is to set up a large well-planted tank. Plenty of cover needs to be provided at the top and bottom of the tank for the babies to hide in. Your adult fish should be placed in this tank. When a female is noticeably gravid she should be removed to a small tank with plenty of plants. This should be done as early in pregnancy as possible to prevent the female giving birth prematurely. Careful netting of the female is essential at this time and it is often best to lift the female out of the tank with the net in a bowl of water. In this way the female does not leave the water and the transfer can be made as gently as possible.

After a brood of fry has been obtained, the female can be returned to the colony tank and the babies reared by themselves for a few weeks. When they are about 1 cm long, one of them can be put back in the colony tank. If the adults leave it alone, then the others can be added. If the single baby is picked on by the adults, then remove it for another week or so before trying again. As the adults become used to small fry in their tank, they will leave new-born young alone unless they are hungry. From then on the colony will maintain itself, with only deformed or weak fish having to be culled when they are seen.

Selective Breeding

In selective breeding the female is always isolated to drop her fry and, as soon as the fry are sexable, the males are removed to a separate tank. This should be done as soon as the rays of the anal fin start to thicken and before the gonopodium is fully formed. In this way, young females remain virgin until you select the male you wish to mate with them. By doing this you are deciding in which direction you want your fish to evolve. If you constantly mate only the biggest and best male with your females, then the line will maintain size and stamina.

One of the problems with this kind of selective breeding of *Xiphophorus* is the fact that young males sex out much earlier when there are no adult males present. To counteract this problem a fully-mature male from the previous generation should be used to mate with the young females. He can be placed in the tank as soon as the fry are large enough not to be harmed by him. He will father the next generation and, at the same time, hold back the development of the young males, so that they have a chance to grow before sexing out. They should still be removed before the gonopodium is fully formed, but this will not happen until the fish are much older and larger than they would be if no adult male were present.

In the cultivated forms, some sort of selective breeding will have to be conducted if the desired characteristics are to be fixed in the strain. Most new strains are developed from an outcross. Normally 2 unrelated fish are mated. As the fry grow any males are removed as soon as they are identified, so that the females will remain virgins. Once they reach breedable size, the best female is selected and mated to the best male. If the father has more of the desirable characteristics than any of his sons then he will be used, if available. This is called *inbreeding* and will be continued through many generations until the strain is breeding pure for the desired characteristics. Sometimes the strain will lose size or develop a fault which cannot be resolved through inbreeding. If this happens then another outcross will have to be made, which will put back the desired genes, and the inbreeding process will have to be started all over again.

Inbreeding Depression

Over the years many myths have grown up around the risks of inbreeding. It has been blamed for everything from poor size to congenital heart conditions and aberrant behaviour. Inbreeding depression is the term used for the decline of a strain due to breeding brother to sister or father to daughter. In fact this close inbreeding is absolutely essential if a strain is to be improved over the generations. More often than not, what aquarists are referring to as 'inbreeding depression' is nothing more than poor selection of breeding stock.

Many aquarists, when they have obtained fry from a female, rear the fry together until they are adult and select the best female from which to save further fry. Unfortunately, the first male to sex out in any litter is the smallest and he will mate with all his sisters, thus perpetuating the genes for small size. A couple of generations of this sort of breeding will result in a small, often weak, strain of fish for which the aquarist blames inbreeding depression. If the aquarist is neglectful, and has not fed the babies properly or given them adequate space for growth, then loss of size will happen in just one generation and be due to stunting rather than the genetic make-up of the fish.

Hybridization

A hybrid is a cross between 2 species of animal or plant. In the wild, very few hybrid *Xiphophorus* have been found. In the 1970s, Dr Kallman reported that, despite over 50,000 platies and swordtails being collected together in the wild, not one single hybrid had been found. However, since that time, several instances of hybridization between wild species have been reported. One of the first of these to be published was by Dr Donn Eric Rosen (1979). This hybridization took place between 2 sympatric species (species which naturally live together) of swordtail – Upland Swordtail and the Green Swordtail.

In 1980, 2 collections of platies from the Rio Purification and Arroyo Chapultepic were brought back to Germany. These were very quickly described as new species: *X. roseni* Meyer & Wischnath, 1981, and *X. kosszanderi* Meyer & Wischnath, 1981. Once these collections had been bred in the aquarium, it soon became clear that they were, in fact, hybrids between the endemic species of platy which had long been known from these locations (the Monterrey Platy in Arroyo Chapultepic and the Spiketail Platy in the Rio Purification) and an introduced Variable Platy. However, although these hybrids were caught in the wild, they should not be referred to as 'naturally-occurring'. This is because the situation at these locations was created by Man and not due to natural conditions.

In the wild, it is very common to find 2 or more species of

Xiphophorus living together but there are certain isolating mechanisms at work which prevent hybridization from occurring. Of these, courtship rituals play an important role as does the occupation by each species of its own particular niche within the river or pond. Another factor which prevents hybridization in the wild is sperm preference. Even if the wrong species does mate with a particular female, then its sperm is most unlikely to be used if the correct sperm is available. All these mechanisms add up to a very effective barrier to hybridization.

In the aquarium, due to the limited space, the isolating mechanisms often fail to work and hybridization can very easily occur. For this reason, it is absolutely essential to maintain each wild *Xiphophorus* species separately from any other *Xiphophorus*. Only in this way can the species be guaranteed pure.

All cultivated platies and swordtails have a hybrid ancestry made up of *X. helleri*, *maculatus* and *variatus* genes in varying degrees, depending upon the strain. Every Wagtail Platy must have *X. helleri* blood in its history because it is a modifier gene from the swordtail which turns a Comet Platy into a Wagtail Platy.

At the present time, few of the wild species have been used in creating new cultivated varieties, but many of these fish have tremendous potential. Most notable among the swordtails is *X. montezumae*, with its extra long sword and black spots. If this could be crossed into a cultivated variety the results might be spectacular. However, the most important thing to remember, when this sort of experimentation is undertaken, is that all rejects from the breeding programme must be culled, or only passed on to other aquarists who are fully aware of their genetic background.

Culling

Culling is the humane disposal of unwanted fish. It is a necessary part of any breeding programme and can be done in a number of ways. For the faint-hearted, a tank can be set aside in which all the deformities and poor-quality fish can live out their lives. This is the soft option and such a tank will soon become overcrowded so that the fish suffer due to the poor conditions.

Another method of abdicating your responsibility is to sell or give away the fish to shops or other aquarists. This will soon give you a bad reputation as an aquarist. At the end of the day the only real solution to the problem of what to do with deformities or other defects is to kill the affected fish. The most humane method is to use an overdose of tranquillizer. Another method is to cool them down in a fridge until they pass away. Many aquarists keep a large predatory fish to eat their culls. Personally, I prefer this method and always keep a few predators in my set-up to perform this necessary function.

9
Cultivated Varieties and Strains

It would be impossible to list all the multitude of cultivated strains which exist in the world today. To give you some idea of how many varieties are possible let us look at the patterns which occur in the wild and then at the combinations which can be created in just one of the 3 species of *Xiphophorus* commonly used in cultivated varieties.

Wild Varieties

Colour Patterns

The colour patterns in the Southern Platy (*X. maculatus*) have been studied in great depth over the years.

Tail-Spot Patterns At least 7 tail-spot patterns are known to exist. These are composed of micromelanophores (small black pigment cells) and are not sex-linked in any way.

- One Spot – A small spot in the middle of the caudal peduncle.
- Twin Spot – Two small spots, one at the top of the caudal peduncle and the other at the bottom.
- Simple Crescent – A simple crescent, as the name would suggest, where the caudal peduncle and caudal fin meet.
- Complete Crescent – The same crescent as the Simple Crescent but an axe-head shape in front of it in the caudal peduncle.
- Simple Moon – One large spot in the middle of the caudal peduncle.
- Mickey Mouse – The same Moon spot with 2 small spots, 1 at the top and 1 at the bottom of the caudal peduncle. This pattern is also called Moon with Satellites and Complete Moon.
- Comet – Black stripes from the caudal peduncle along the top and bottom edge of the caudal fin.

Macromelanophore Patterns Other kinds of patterning in the Southern Platy are known and these are made up of macromelanophores (large black pigment cells). They are partially sex-linked and produce some of the more spectacular colour patterns. At least 5 of these are known:

- Spotted – Black spots all over the body.

- Spotted Dorsal – Large black spots in the dorsal fin, usually concentrated towards the base.
- Striped – Black stripes along the flanks made up of spots running into each other.
- Black-banded – Thick black bands which run into each other, covering much of the flanks.
- Black Belly – Black spots running into each other and concentrated in the ventral region.

Red and Yellow Patterns   Various patterns of these pigments are also known:

- Red Body – Whole of the body and fins are red.
- Yellow Body – Whole of the body and fins are yellow.
- Red Dorsal – Base of the dorsal fin is deep red, fading towards the edge of the fin and sometimes spreading into the body.
- Red Anal – Anal and pelvic fins are red throughout.
- Ruby Throat – Red throat and a number of vertical red lines along the flanks. This wild coloration was used to create the Bleeding Heart Platy.

Cultivated Varieties

One of the interesting things about all these different wild patterns is that they can often be combined in order to create a new colour pattern. This pattern is not always just the sum of the 2, 3 or more wild colour patterns used in its creation but sometimes a micromelanophore pattern will affect the way a macromelanophore pattern is expressed. Dr Gordon (1928) reported on such a case.

He selected 2 genes for this study. One was a dominant gene for stippling. (This is a micromelanophore pattern which covers the fish in small dots over its whole body.) The other was for the macromelanophore pattern for spots. (This is a dominant sex-linked gene which produces large spots over the whole of the fish.)

One parent had both genes whilst the other had neither. In the F2 generation, 4 types of fish were produced. One of the new types had the spotted gene without the stippling gene and the other had the stippling gene without the spotted gene. Those fish with the spotted gene but not the stippling gene had far fewer spots, so the stippling gene enhanced the effect of the spotted gene. However, those fish with the stippling gene but not the spotted gene had far more stipples, so the spotted gene inhibited the effect of the stippling gene.

In his book *Enjoy your Platys and Swordtails*, Dr Kallman estimated that there were at least 363,264 different colour patterns possible in the

Southern Platy without using other *Xiphophorus* species for hybridization. Once you start to use the other species you are talking in the millions and you have the added variation of with or without the sword!!

Certain fancy-fin varieties and colour patterns in *Xiphophorus* have become established over the decades and I shall list some of these and give some pointers as to what to look for both when selecting breeding-stock and judging these fish.

Colour Varieties

The following are the main colour varieties commonly seen.

Albino In this colour variety there is no black pigmentation. This means the eye is pink and so, usually, is the body. When combined with Red you obtain a Red-eyed Red which, in the Velvet form, is a deep blood-red all over. The Albino gene is recessive to most other colours.

Black This coloration can come in several different forms. In a true Black the whole body of the fish is black except for the throat and head. In some strains each scale has an iridescent green sheen to it. These are often known as Hamburg Crosses. Cancers are common in many strains of black *Xiphophorus* and are particularly prevalent in fish with black finnage.

Xiphophorus helleri. Male Black Swordtail. This fish has good colour and with the clear finnage is less likely to develop cancer as it grows older. However, the sword is very short and bent upwards towards the end. This can be a genetic fault but it is more likely that the sword has been damaged and grown back short and bent.

Bleeding Heart In the late 1930s Dr Myron Gordon found a wild *X. maculatus* with a red throat in the Rio Jamapa. This he crossed with a White Ghost Platy and selectively bred until the new strain was fixed. This he called the Bleeding Heart Platy because the coloration suggested that the heart of the fish had burst and the blood had ran down the sides of the body to collect in the chest region. The strain was exhibited for the first time in 1948 at the New York Aquarium and was soon well established in the hobby. Unfortunately, only the males exhibited the colour pattern at this time but, through careful selective breeding, the female in certain strains now exhibits the colour pattern; unfortunately, males from these strains often exhibit an intensified red pattern which loses the true Bleeding Heart pattern. This is one of the real tests of cultivated livebearer breeding – just as you take 1 step forward you often take 2 back as well!

When selecting breeders and judging fish of this strain, look for a good, clean colour pattern and as few fine black spots on the body as possible. The black spotting is part-and-parcel of the Bleeding Heart pattern at the moment and, whilst efforts are being made to eliminate it, such fish should not be heavily penalized until this has been achieved.

Xiphophorus maculatus. Male Bleeding Heart Platy. This fish has the true Bleeding Heart colour pattern, although the red is somewhat lacking on the ventral surface of this fish.

Xiphophorus maculatus. Male from the Bleeding Heart Platy strain which produces females with the Bleeding Heart pattern. In this fish, the Bleeding Heart pattern has extended to cover nearly the whole body. Whilst very attractive, it is no longer a true 'Bleeding Heart Platy'.

Blue   Blue *Xiphophorus* have a bluish body overlaid by iridescent blue scales. This is usually combined with a tail-spot pattern and clear fins. However, a rare strain of Variable Platy has an iridescent blue-to-purple body, becoming red towards the caudal peduncle and throughout the caudal fin. This is overlaid by many black spots throughout the body. All the other fins are yellow. This is a very attractive strain which is almost impossible to obtain now.

Comet   This coloration refers to a black streak in the upper and lower caudal peduncle and caudal fin. It can be seen on most body colours and comes from a wild platy strain. This coloration is also called Twin-bar.

Ghost   In this coloration the body of the fish is pure white with clear fins. The eye is still black so it is not an Albino.

Gold   This is one of the oldest colours but one which seems to be quite rare now. The whole body of the fish is an intense yellow-gold with a yellow coloration into the finnage. A pale gold or almost white form is also known.

Hawaiian In this colour form the body is jet black along the back and sides with yellow on the under-abdomen. The dorsal fin is lemon-yellow and the caudal fin bright red. Selecting adult breeders presents no problems, but, if you need to cull the youngsters on the grounds of colour, do not keep the darkest black individuals as these will turn all-black and have clear fins. The fish to rear-on are those with black speckling only along the sides. As these grow, the black coloration will spread until the whole of the sides are black. The finnage coloration will still be very variable and only those fish with the best coloration should be used as breeders.

Leopard The basic body coloration is yellow but this is overlaid by blue and mauve. The caudal is bright red with this colour extending into the caudal peduncle. The dorsal fin is lemon-yellow with an even black border. The whole body of the fish is overlaid with black spots, which should be as evenly spread as possible.

Xiphophorus variatus. Male Hawaiian normal-fin platy. This male has excellent colour and would be suitable for breeding stock.

Xiphophorus variatus. Male Leopard Variatus Platy. A very nice fish with good colour.

Red Red *Xiphophorus* come in 2 forms: Brick Red and Velvet Red. In Brick Red, the red coloration is more orange than red, whilst Velvet Red is an intense blood-red. Either coloration is acceptable on the show bench although the Velvet Red is generally preferred. One of the most important points to check when judging either of these types is that the coloration extends over the whole of the body (white throats are a common fault) and reaches to the extremities of the finnage. The Velvet Red strains are sometimes called Coral Red.

Red Jet Fish exhibiting this coloration are sometimes called Frankfurt Crosses. In this coloration the front half of the body is red and the rear half jet black. These fish often continue to develop black pigmentation throughout their lives and are particularly susceptible to cancer in later life. This is probably why such an attractive strain has never become common in the hobby.

Salt and Pepper This coloration was very popular about a decade ago but has become scarce in more recent times. The whole body of the fish is covered with fine black spots on a white background. Yellow and orange backgrounds are also known. The coloration is always more intense in males than females and tends to be concentrated towards the rear of the fish. The more desirable fish are those with an evenness of marking throughout the body and fins.

Xiphophorus helleri. Red-eyed Red Swordtail female. The colour could be a little more intense on this fish. The white throat which is so common on many Red Swordtails has been bred out of this strain.

Xiphophorus maculatus. A male Velvet Red or Coral Red Platy. This fish has fine colour and a good body shape but it has a very slight caudal appendage.

Xiphophorus helleri. Male Brick-red Red-eyed Swordtail. This fish has a good sword development, reasonable colour and a good body shape. Unfortunately it is only some 5 cm in body length and fully sexed out. An outcross will be needed to restore the size on this strain. The brick-red coloration is not so popular as the velvet-red.

Sunset, Sunburst or Marigold   This is commonly associated with Variable Platies. The ground colour is yellow, becoming orange towards the rear of the body and a deep blood-red in the caudal fin. All other fins are yellow.

Tiger   This has the same coloration as the Sunburst except that the body is overlaid with 4–6 vertical bars like tiger-stripes.

Tricolour   These fish have the same Sunset body coloration but the fins exhibit the Wagtail pattern. Dr Joanne Norton made this coloration famous with her beautiful Tricolour Plumetail Maculatus Platies.

Tuxedo   In this colour form the body may be any colour overlaid with a large triangular black mark. The apex of this is near the eye, whilst the base is the caudal peduncle.

Xiphophorus variatus. Male Sunburst or Marigold Lyretail Platy. The extended gonopodium of this male is clearly visible. The front rays of the dorsal fin are bent, which may be a genetic fault or the result of damage. The top lobe of the caudal extension has also been damaged and will not grow back straight.

Wagtail   In this colour pattern all the fins and the lips are black. Ideally this should be a deep velvety black to the extremities of the fins. Because this coloration demands the combination of a swordtail and a platy gene, all Wagtails must be of hybrid origin at some point in their ancestry.

Fancy-fin Varieties

Hi-fin   Hi-fin *Xiphophorus* have been known for over 30 years now. The first fish of this type was discovered by Mr and Mrs Thomas Simpson of Gardena, California. This fish and the subsequent generations had long, narrow, dorsal fins with few if any branching rays; all other fins were normal. Over the decades, modifiers were bred into Hi-fins which caused the dorsal fin rays to branch until the fin on a good male resembled a sail trailing beyond the caudal peduncle. As yet, the inheritance of these modifying factors is not fully understood but, when selecting breeding-stock, choose fish with fins which have rays with as many branches as possible.

The females of this variety do not have the middle rays of the dorsal fin extended to the same degree as the males. This means the leading rays stand up higher than the others, giving the fin a pointed shape.

So far, it seems that all Hi-fin *Xiphophorus* carry the gene for normal fin. This is because the Hi-fin gene is lethal in fish when it occurs twice (homozygous) and embryos with this genetic make-up die whilst *in utero*. Since the Hi-fin gene is dominant when Hi-fin is crossed to normal-fin, the offspring are 50 per cent Hi-fin and 50 per cent normal-fin. When 2 Hi-fins are mated, the offspring are 66 per cent Hi-fin and 33 per cent normal-fin. However, these percentages do not truly represent what has happened to all the brood. What we really have is 25 per cent normal-fin, 50 per cent Hi-fin and 25 per cent dead. Even the Hi-fins which are born are weaker than their normal-fin siblings and will grow more slowly and be more susceptible to disease.

When judging fish with this characteristic, extra credit should be given to those fish with many branching rays and an allowance should be made for deportment. It would be unreasonable to expect any fish with such a huge fin to hold it erect all the time and the judging should reflect this.

Xiphophorus helleri. A beautiful male Red Hi-fin Lyretail Swordtail. Its only fault is the white throat.

Xiphophorus maculatus. Yellow Wagtail Hi-fin Platy. In this fish the dorsal fin could be a little more evenly developed with a somewhat more intense black coloration. However, on such a large fin, the black pigmentation can never be as intense as it is on the normal-finned types.

Xiphophorus variatus. A beautiful male Hi-fin Sunset Variatus Platy.

Lyretail   This gene was discovered in a fish at Don Adam's fish-farm in Florida. It has the effect of elongating all the fins and extending the leading rays into threads. The upper and lower rays of the caudal fin are also elongated. Since the dorsal fin is enlarged somewhat, the name 'Hi-fin Lyretail' is often used for these fish but, despite the name, they do not generally have the Hi-fin gene. If they do, the whole of the dorsal fin is enlarged in exactly the same way as the true Hi-fin. Because of the extension of the male's gonopodium, it is impossible for him to mate. Even if this fin is cut down to the right length, it is still impossible for him to mate successfully with a female because the hook and claw on the end of the gonopodium, which allow him to latch onto the female during mating, are not present. For this reason a normal-fin male must be used to keep the strain going. A Hi-fin male may be used to produce true Hi-fin Lyretails, but this combination so weakens the fish that few such strains can be maintained in the long term. If you do decide to work with this combination, then it is wise to keep extra Hi-fins and Lyretails so that the strain can be reconstituted if need be.

Xiphophorus variatus. Female Hawaiian Lyretail Platy. This female has good colour and, at 7.5 cm body length, good size. Its faults are a short top lobe to the caudal fin and a slight fault in the body shape along the dorsal surface. Whilst not a bad fault in this fish, careful selection of its offspring will be essential if a bad body shape is not to become fixed in this strain.

Xiphophorus variatus. Female Leopard Lyretail Platy. This fish could have deeper colour and both the top lobe of the caudal fin and the dorsal-fin extension are a little short but it is still suitable as breeding-stock if nothing better is available. The body length of this female is nearly 7.5 cm.

When selecting breeding stock or judging Lyretails, fish with equal extensions, particularly on the caudal fin, should be given preference. However, a slight extension in the middle of the caudal fin is acceptable as this is a natural part of the Lyretail gene.

When a Lyretail's finnage is damaged it will grow back ragged. In extreme cases this will cause the entire fin to extend into a veil. This sometimes happens after a heavy infestation with velvet disease or whitespot when all the edges of the fins are damaged. In such cases 'Veiltails' are produced where all the fins are extended. These fish can look very spectacular and, occasionally, a fish-farmer has been known to deliberately chop off the ends of the fins to create a 'Veiltail' strain. In this way he can sell the same fish for a much higher price. Unfortunately, when these fish are bred from, the young are Lyretails.

Plumetail, Brushtail & Pintail This gene first occurred in a German aquarist's tank. These fish were then sold to a pet-shop from where the Zoological Institute of the University of Hamburg obtained them. They made their way back into hobbyists' tanks via Mr Entlinger, who obtained them sometime in the late 1960s.

There is a great deal of variation in this genetic type, depending on what the breeder has been selecting for. The Plumetail or Brushtail type has a long, many-pronged extension in the middle of the caudal fin. In the Pintail this extension comes to a fine point. The same gene is operating in each case but modifiers change the fin from Pintail to Plumetail. This is supposedly a dominant gene that is autosomal in nature (i.e. not carried on the sex chromosomes). Its inheritance seems a little confused but true-breeding strains are available now.

When selecting breeders or judging this strain, preference should be given to fish which exhibit one or other finnage type. If you are breeding a Plumetail strain then the plume should be wide, long and many-pronged whereas, in a Pintail, it should come to a fine point; in-between fish should not be included in the breeding-programme. Fish of both types tend to exhibit a prong or small sword on the bottom of the caudal fin. This is a normal characteristic of this fish.

We have deliberately left out the terms platy and swordtail in the above descriptions as all colour varieties and fin types can be found in fish which look like *X. helleri*, *maculatus* or *variatus*. However, such scientific names for these cultivated hybrids do not really apply as just about every cultivated fish is of hybrid origin.

Xiphophorus maculatus. A magnificent female Tricolour Plumetail Platy bred by Dr Joanne Norton.

When selecting breeders for body shape and normal finnage, fish exhibiting characteristics closest to 1 of the 3 basic types should be looked for. This is particularly true when an outcross has been made to create a new strain, or fresh blood has been added to an established strain. The same should be true when judging, although recently a new form of Variatus Platy was created by one of the Florida fish-farmers. In this fish, the body shape and coloration was that of the classic Variatus Platy but the males exhibited a short upcurved sword. Whether this half-way house will become popular remains to be seen; however, it is certainly true that the work of the cultivationist goes on and many new colour forms and fin types are yet to be created.

Improving an Established Strain

We all have to start with a cultivated strain somewhere and often the initial stock we obtain is lacking in some important way. With swordtails this is often size and sword length. There are 2 ways to improve this. Firstly, you should obtain your first generation of young and rear them in your own conditions. This will often improve size and with it sword length. If the fish still fail to achieve a good size then it is probably because of the genes that the strain is carrying. To solve this problem you will need to do what is called an *outcross*.

The Outcross

An outcross occurs when an unrelated or distantly-related fish is crossed into an established strain to introduce a desirable characteristic that was never there or had been lost. To best explain the benefits and pitfalls of this procedure we will use several examples from our personal experience.

Our initial stock of Red-eyed Red Sword were very poor in size, colour and sword length. After a few generations we had managed to breed them into a good velvet-red colour and eliminate the white throat but the size and sword length remained poor. To correct this, we used a male, from a wild population of Green Swordtail from Lake Catemaco, which had an extremely long sword and good body size. The first generation babies were all green, as was expected. The sword length and body size were greatly improved. The latest sexing-out male which achieved the largest size was mated back into the Red-eyed Red strain and the following offspring were produced: 25 per cent Red, 25 per cent Green, 25 per cent Albino and 25 per cent Red-eyed Red. By selecting the best Red-eyed Red pair from these offspring, we returned to a true-breeding strain of fish which had a much improved sword length and good body size.

Creating a New Cultivated Strain

All cultivated strains of fish start in 1 of 2 ways: an idea or an accident. In the case of an idea, the aquarist looks at 2 strains of fish and thinks 'I wonder what would happen if I crossed this, with that?' or 'Wouldn't that strain look beautiful if it had red fins?' These sorts of ideas have led to the creation of some beautiful strains of cultivated fish. The other way for a new strain of cultivated fish to be created is by accident. These accidents fall into 2 groups: genetic and aquaristic. Genetic accidents are called *sports* and they can happen at any time and in any aquarist's tanks. All the fancy-fin types are examples of sports which just turned up out of the blue. The aquaristic accidents are those mistakes which happen from time to time even in a good aquarist's tanks, where a fish jumps from one tank to another and mates with the wrong strain. These accidents have sometimes produced really worthwhile fish but, by then, the aquarist concerned usually tells everybody it was a planned experiment!

Whichever way a strain starts life, nothing will remove the hard work needed over a period of many years to refine and fix the strain so that it will breed relatively true. To accomplish this, careful selective inbreeding needs to be undertaken over a period of many generations to eliminate those genes which are not wanted in the strain and to enhance the effect of those genes which are wanted. All too often, writers wander off into the realms of theoretical breeding-charts at this point and complicate things unnecessarily. We have already discussed improving a cultivated strain through the use of an outcross. In the process, we created 2 new strains of swordtail. One was an Albino and the other a Red. Fixing either of these strains would have been quite easy. By mating 2 fish of either colour together, it would have been quite easy to inbreed brother and sister together until we had a true breeding strain of one or the other.

However, after our initial success, we decided to try a new outcross to introduce the Lyretail gene into the strain. A good Red-eyed Red Lyretail is an attractive fish and very rare. For our initial cross, we obtained a female Red Lyretail from a friend who had been working with the strain for many generations. The size and finnage were good so we hoped for some excellent results. The first offspring were all Red fish and 50 per cent were Lyretails. This was exactly as expected. The best female Lyretail from these offspring was mated back to our best male Red-eyed Red. Once again the statistics worked out exactly, with 50 per cent of the young being Lyretails and 50 per cent normals. Coloration was again as expected, with 50 per cent Red and 50 per cent Red-eyed Red; this meant that 25 per cent of the brood were Red-eyed Red Lyretails. These were isolated from the normal-finned Red-eyed Reds so that the females would remain virgin since male Lyretails are incapable of breeding. The normal-fin Red-eyed Reds from this brood were kept in a separate tank and the old strain was sold off to make way for our newly-created Red-eyed Red Lyretail strain. It was at this point that disaster struck. The normal-finned fish died off for no apparent reason. However, we still had about 25 young Lyretails which could be crossed to any swordtail to re-establish the line. Then the second disaster struck. All the Lyretails sexed out as males. Because these were unable to mate on account of the extended gonopodium, the strain died out.

Our biggest mistake was to phase out the old strain before we were sure that we had not introduced any problems with the outcross. It is also wise to work with 2 lines of the same strain. This can be achieved easily when you first obtain a new strain. When we first obtained the Red-eyed Red strain and made the outcross with the Green Swordtail, we should have kept the best 2 pairs of Red-eyed Reds and established separate lines from them. Then we could have worked on just 1 line when trying to introduce the Lyretail gene. We would then have had the other line to fall back on when the outcross failed. The other important aspect to having 2 lines of the same strain is that you can use each line as an outcross for the other if size or vitality seems to be deteriorating. This way you are using fish of a known genetic make-up which are less likely to cause problems.

10
Wild Platy and Swordtail Species

Xiphophorus alvarezi
Rosen, 1960
Upland Swordtail

Taxonomic Details
First described by Donn E. Rosen (1960) in 'Middle-American poeciliid fishes of the genus *Xiphophorus*' *Bull. Fla St. Mus. Biol. Sci.* **5** (4): 57–242.

ETYMOLOGY The species was named for Sr José Alvarez del Villar who was the Secretario de Marina in Mexico and passed on specimens of this species to Donn Eric Rosen who named the fish.

SYNONYMS *X. helleri alvarezi* Rosen, 1960

SPECIES-GROUP 3

TYPE LOCALITY Rio Santo Domingo, which is a tributary of the Rio Jatate in the upper reaches of the Rio Usumacinta system, Chiapas, Mexico. The type specimens were collected by M. del Toro in August 1948 at a collecting site some 90 km east of Comitán. It has been estimated that this location is approximately 500 m above sea level. The holotype is a 39 mm SL male and the allotype is a 39.4 mm SL female.

Distribution
Mexico: This species is found in the intermontane and upland basins of the Sierras in Chiapas. Guatemala: Huehuetenango, El Quiche and Alta Verapaz, in the Rio Usumacinta watershed.

Description
The Upland Swordtail has a single, red, mid-lateral stripe which is always developed into a solid band. Occasionally, there is another red stripe above the mid-lateral stripe which is separated by a band of blue. In certain populations there may be more red stripes along the sides and a yellow to orange coloration on the lower sides of the body. The dorsal fin has 2 rows of red spots and the sword of the male is yellow edged in black. This coloration is similar to a number of populations of the much better-known Green Swordtail (*X. helleri*). There are a number of different populations of the Upland Swordtail (most notably the Guatemalan ones) which may be a new species in their own right and are under investigation at the moment. The male lodged in the Natural History Museum was collected with the type series and has the following measurements: 43 mm SL; 10 mm BD maximum, 8 mm minimum; sword 50 mm. The multi-striped Guatemalan form tends to be deeper in the body and have a shorter sword.

SIZE Males: 60 mm. Females: 75 mm.

Xiphophorus alvarezi. Male from Rio Santo Domingo, Chiapas State, Mexico.

Temperament, Care and Breeding

The Upland Swordtail comes from rivers with a good current and plenty of plant growth. In captivity, it does best in a well-planted aquarium with either filtration or large, regular, partial water-changes. It is a shy, nervous species which likes to be in a large group. When the female is near to term, it is wise to remove her to another aquarium in which there is plenty of plant cover, so that the fry will not be harmed by the other fish. If they are well fed, it is possible to breed this fish in a natural colony situation. However, the natural colony set-up does not appear to be as successful with this species as it is with many of the other Xiphophorines.

Xiphophorus andersi
Meyer & Schartl, 1980
Anders Platy

Taxonomic Details

First described by M. K. Meyer and M. Schartl (1980) in 'Eine neue *Xiphophorus*-Art aus Vera Cruz, Mexico' *Senckenberg. Biol.* **60** (3–4): 147–51.

ETYMOLOGY The species was named for Professor Dr F. Anders.

SYNONYMS None

SPECIES-GROUP 2

TYPE LOCALITY Rio Atoyac by Finca St Anita, near the town of Chico in the state of Veracruz, Mexico. This collection was made on 24 February 1979 by E. Hnilicka. The type specimen is a 33.6 mm SL male.

Distribution
Mexico: So far, this species is only known from the type locality.

Description
This is a relatively drably-coloured, slender platy species whose males have a short sword. There are 2 size morphs in males of this species, with the large morph showing a pseudo-gravidity spot above the gonopodium. The body has an overall brownish coloration, becoming dirty white in front of the gravid spot. The fins are brown with several darker crescents in the dorsal fin of both sexes.

SIZE Males: 25 mm and 40 mm, depending on size morph. Females: 75 mm.

Temperament, Care and Breeding
This is a peaceful species which does well in most conditions. A well-planted tank with good filtration suits them ideally; alternatively large, regular, partial water-changes should be undertaken. In the wild, this fish lives near the banks of a fast-flowing river. If the adults are well fed, it is possible to breed this species in a natural colony situation, in which case, males will sex out more slowly and achieve a greater adult size.

Xiphophorus andersi. Male from Rio Atoyac, Veracruz State, Mexico. Regular size morph.

Xiphophorus birchmanni
Lechner & Radda, 1987
Sheepshead Swordtail

Taxonomic Details
First described by P. Lechner and A. C. Radda (1987) in 'Revision des *Xiphophorus montezumae/cortezi*-Komplexes und Neubeschreibung einer Sunspezies. St. Gallen, Switzerland' *Aquaria* **34**: 189–96.

ETYMOLOGY This species was named for one of the collectors, H. Birchmann.

SYNONYMS *X. montezumae birchmanni* Lechner & Radda, 1987

SPECIES-GROUP 3

CLADE Cortezi

TYPE LOCALITY Rio Talol, in the state of Hidalgo, Mexico, which is a headwater of the Rio San Pedro. This river in turn flows into the Rio Tempoal and finally into the Rio Panuco itself. The holotype is a male some 60 mm in length collected by P. Lechner and H. Birchmann on 27 April 1987.

Distribution
Mexico: This species is found throughout the southern region of the Rio Panuco basin and in the headwaters of the Rio Tuxpan. In some areas of its distribution it is found with the Cortes Swordtail and Highland Swordtail and whether hybrids are found in nature is still under investigation. Where the Sheepshead Swordtail occurs in the same river system as Cortes Swordtail,

Xiphophorus birchmanni. Male from Rio Calabozo collection. This male clearly exhibits the very short sword which some males of this species have.

it will generally be found at higher elevations. However, when it occurs with the Highland Swordtail, it will be found at lower elevations.

Description

The unusual common name is derived from the large knobbly hump on the head of mature males. This is similar to the hump of the Hump-back Limia (*Limia nigrofasciata*) and is not a fault. Two more characteristics of this species distinguish it from the other 2 members of the clade. Firstly, the males, and to a lesser degree the females, have very broad vertical bars along the sides. In the Cortes Swordtail, these are fine whilst in the Highland Swordtail they are more distinct but often broken into blotches. Finally, and most importantly, the Sheepshead Swordtail male has hardly any sword at all. In wild populations less than 1 per cent of the males have any sword appendage. In the aquarium the percentage seems to be higher but the sword is never more than a short spike of about 5 mm length.

Members of the Cortezi clade of Rio Panuco basin swordtails are characterized by a single zigzag lateral stripe running from the eye to the caudal peduncle. In females this is always clearly shown, but in males this is only visible when the fish is young or not sexually active.

SIZE Males: 50 mm. Females: 50 mm.

Temperament, Care and Breeding

This species is rather shy in the aquarium, preferring to hide amongst the plants. However, if there is a large mixed age-group of fish in the tank, it will become less timid. Broods are born on a 28-day cycle and average about 30 in number for an adult female. The fry are easy to rear and it is possible to breed this fish in a natural colony situation if enough cover is provided and the adults are well fed.

Xiphophorus clemenciae
Alvarez, 1959
Yellow Swordtail

Taxonomic Details

First described by J. Alvarez (1959) in 'Nuevas especies de *Xiphophorus* e *Hyporhamphus* procedents del Rio Coatzacoalcos' *Cienc. Mex.* **19**: 69–73.

ETYMOLOGY This species was named for the wife of J. Alvarez, Clemencia Alvarez.

SYNONYMS None

SPECIES-GROUP 3

TYPE LOCALITY Arroyo La Cascada, which is a headwater of the Rio Sarabia on the Ranch of San Carlos some 24 km east of Palomares in the state of Oaxaca, Mexico. The type series was collected by José Alvarez on 26 May 1959. The holotype is a male 30 mm SL and the allotype a female 39.2 mm SL. Dr Miller, who collected this species before Alvarez but overlooked the new swordtail due to its similarity to the common Green Swordtail, reports that the habitat had clear water with no vegetation. The bottom consisted of mud, silt and brush. The stream was only about 1.3 m wide and was bordered by dense tropical rainforest. The current was moderate to almost non-existent in March 1957 but, in February 1959, the stream was a raging torrent and the Yellow Swordtail was present in greater numbers.

Distribution

Mexico: The Yellow Swordtail was always thought to be limited to the

Xiphophorus clemenciae. Male from Puente Chinoluiz, Oaxaca State, Mexico. Wild-caught fish.

headwaters of the Rio Sarabia and down to its confluence with the Rio Coatzacoalcos. However, Dr Klaus Kallman has now found this species to be much more widespread than was originally thought and it may well occur in most small tributaries of upper reaches of the Rio Coatzacoalcos but not generally in the main river itself.

I have found this fish in a tributary of the Rio Coatzacoalcos 9 km from the town of Sarabia along a road signposted 'Uxpanapa'. The road goes over a small bridge with a hand-painted sign saying 'Puente Chinoluiz' and the stream flows under this.

Description
This is one of the loveliest of all the small swordtails. In body form it is similar to the well-known Green Swordtail although the caudal peduncle is somewhat deeper. The body is greenish blue with 2 intense red stripes running its full length. The lower runs from the eye to the top of the sword whilst the upper runs parallel to this, 1 scale row higher. On some collections there may be up to 4 red lines. Just above the pelvic fins, a black stripe starts and runs along the side of the fish and eventually ends up as the black lower edge of the sword. The top of the sword is also black whilst the middle is an intense lemon-yellow. Alvarez reported that some males were an intense yellow in the wild and it was from this coloration that the common name of Yellow Swordtail was derived.

SIZE Males: 50 mm. Females: 55 mm.

Temperament, Care and Breeding
For many years the Yellow Swordtail has been top of the list of desirable species for livebearer enthusiasts throughout Europe. However, it has also been just about unobtainable

since its only known collecting-sites were very difficult to reach or the fish was only very rarely found.

The Yellow Swordtail has the reputation of being extremely difficult to maintain, with small broods of weak, tiny young being produced erratically. However, when we discussed this fish with American aquarists who had maintained it some years ago, we were told it was just as easy to breed as the Green Swordtail and they could not understand what all the fuss was over! Such a divergence of opinion over the same fish can often be accounted for by misidentification but this was not the case in this instance.

Our own experience with this species comes from a collection made in 1992 from one of the new collecting-sites. At this location, the water was shallow and slow-moving, with limited aquatic plant growth. The water quality was hard and slightly alkaline and there was an abundance of other fish. These included *X. helleri*, *Priapella intermedia*, *Poeciliopsis gracilis*, *Cichlasoma aureum*, *C. fenestratum* and *Astynax* sp. The 3 males and 5 females collected at this site were placed in a 60 cm × 25 cm tank with some cover, as the males sparred with each other from time to time, although no real damage was done.

Within a month of capture, the females started to reproduce. Broods were born every 25–31 days and numbered from 5 for a small female's first brood up to 60 for a fully-adult female. These were normally born during the day and females often picked at the fry if they were not removed soon after they had finished giving birth.

Xiphophorus clemenciae. Female from Puente Chinoluiz, Oaxaca State, Mexico. Wild-caught fish.

The fry were small but would eat newly-hatched Brine Shrimps within a few hours of being born and grew well on this diet. Our adults were fed on a mixed diet of 2 feeds of live baby Brine Shrimps plus 1 feed of flake food per day. No additional vegetable matter was added to the diet.

After a good number of fry had been collected by separating the gravid females we allowed a female to drop fry in the colony tank. Although some of these were eaten, a reasonable number survived, so it is possible to breed this species in a natural colony situation. Females which are just about to give birth develop a larger and darker gravid spot, together with a squared-off appearance to their bodies.

It is possible that the divergence in opinion about this fish was due to different collections behaving differently in captivity. Alternatively, the few people who worked with this species may have had very different set-ups, which led to 2 such extreme views. Our own stocks have reproduced very well with many hundreds of babies having been reared to maturity over the last year.

Xiphophorus continens
Rauchenberger, Kallman & Morizot, 1990
El Quince Swordtail

Taxonomic Details
First described by Mary Rauchenberger, Klaus Kallman and Donald C. Morizot (1990) in 'Monophyly and geography of the Rio Panuco Basin swordtails (genus *Xiphophorus*) with descriptions of four new species' *Am. Mus. Novit.* No. 2975: 41 pp.

ETYMOLOGY The scientific name comes from the Greek *conto* = 'short', and the Latin *ensis* = 'sword', which is a reference to the very small sword which males of this species have.

The common name of El Quince Swordtail comes from the tiny little village at the end of the 'road' which you have to drive along in order to be within walking-distance of the type locality. It is very doubtful that a normal car would be able to reach this location because the road is no more than a track through the sugar-cane fields. It winds on for over 30 km and, from time to time, the mud is so deep that even the bottom of a minibus scrapes the ground. At the end of the drive comes a trek through the fields and undergrowth to the *nacimiento* of the Rio Ojo Frio. This spring has beautiful, crystal-clear water tinged with blue and teaming with fish. An absolutely wonderful location if you can survive the journey!

SYNONYMS *Xiphophorus* sp. nov. Zimmer & Kallman, 1988

SPECIES-GROUP 3

CLADE Montezumae

TYPE LOCALITY The headwater springs of the Rio Ojo Frio at the village of El Quince, north of Damian Carmona, in the state of San Luis Potosí, Mexico. The holotype is a male 20 mm SL collected by K. D. Kallman and D. C. Morizot on 27 April 1984.

Distribution
Mexico: So far, this species is only known from the headwaters of the Rio Ojo Frio north of the town of Damian Carmona.

Description
The El Quince Swordtail looks very much like *X. pygmaeus* but shares far more derived characteristics with the *montezumae–nezahualcoyotl* group. This is borne out, to a certain extent,

Xiphophorus continens. Male from El Quince in the state of San Luis Potosí, Mexico. First-generation young from wild-caught fish.

Xiphophorus continens. Female from El Quince, San Luis Potosí State, Mexico. First-generation young from wild-caught fish. Females of this species look very similar to female *X. montezumae.*

by my own experiences when looking at this species in the wild. Every catch contained large numbers of Montezuma Swordtails as well as El Quince Swordtails and differentiating between them when they were about 15 mm long was a real problem. It would have been even more difficult had we not possessed a clear-sided container to examine them in.

Both sexes of the El Quince Swordtail have a dark lateral stripe composed of zigzags which run from the eye into the caudal peduncle. There are a further 1 or 2 less distinct stripes above and below the prominent one. The sword in males is no more than 1 mm long and adult males achieve a size of only 25 mm at maximum. The females are reported to grow as large as Northern Mountain Swordtail females but I have not seen any larger than 35 mm, even in the wild.

Despite extensive sampling since 1984, no gold-morph males of this species have ever been found in the wild nor occurred in captive-bred populations.

SIZE Males: 25 mm. Females: 35 mm.

Temperament, Care and Breeding

We are still in the early days with this species but so far it has proven to be peaceful and easy to keep in the aquarium. In the wild it is found in areas of heavy plant growth, so some cover in the aquarium is appreciated, although once settled it will frequently be seen swimming around at the front of the tank looking for food. As it is found at a fairly high altitude, cooler temperatures of approximately 21–22°C are more suitable for this species. Broods have, so far, numbered up to 20 and are born on a monthly cycle at a temperature of 22°C. If the adults are well fed it is possible to breed this species in a natural colony situation.

Xiphophorus cortezi
Rosen, 1960
Cortes Swordtail

Taxonomic Details

First described by Donn E. Rosen (1960) in 'Middle-American poeciliid fishes of the genus *Xiphophorus*' *Bull. Fla St. Mus., Biol. Sci.* **5** (4): 57–242.

ETYMOLOGY This species was named after Hernan Cortes (1485–1547), who in 1519 sailed from Cuba via Cozumel to Mexico with 11 ships, 100 sailors and 508 soldiers. Three years later Cortez was appointed governor of New Spain and, by 1524, he had conquered nearly the whole of the Aztec Empire as far south as Honduras and El Salvador.

SYNONYMS *X. montezumae cortezi* Rosen, 1960

SPECIES-GROUP 3

CLADE Cortezi

TYPE LOCALITY Arroyo Matlapa at Comoca, 3.2 km north of Axtla, Rio Panuco basin in the state of San Luis Potosí, Mexico. The type series was collected by Myron Gordon, S. Coronad and H. F. Gandy on 14–15 April 1939. The holotype is a male 38.5 mm SL and the allotype a female 34.9 mm SL.

Distribution

Mexico: This species is fairly widespread south of the Rio Tampaon, being found in the Rios Choy, Moctezuma, Axtla, San Pedro and Candelaria. It prefers streams with a good current and rocky bottoms with plenty of boulders to hide under. In the headwaters of Rio Tancuilin at Rio Verdito, in the state of Queretaro, this species has been collected in water with a temperature of only 13°C.

Xiphophorus cortezi. Male from the Rio Axtla.

Description

The Cortes Swordtail has a single black zigzag stripe which runs from the eye to the caudal peduncle. Above this, the body is brownish yellow with each scale edged in dark brown to give a net-like appearance. Below the lateral stripe the body is whitish yellow. In the male the sword is black-edged and somewhat upturned in most specimens. The large sail-like dorsal fin is lemon-yellow with black spots. The other fins are clear to yellowish with the sword yellow edged in black. Occasionally, males are seen with large areas of black and gold on them. When in breeding colour, males exhibit fine vertical bars along the sides.

Two male size morphs of this species have been identified, but this only becomes apparent when they are raised in mass culture. Under such conditions, the large-morph males are up to 10 mm larger than the small-morph fish.

SIZE Males: 50 mm. Females: 50 mm.

Temperament, Care and Breeding

The Cortes Swordtail is a peaceful, attractive swordtail which will live happily in a community tank of average-sized aquarium inhabitants. If enough plant cover is provided, some fry will even survive to maturity in such conditions.

Feeding represents no problem as it will take all foods ravenously. Whilst being quite tolerant to temperature, an average of 22°C should be aimed for. Higher temperatures will tend to speed up maturation and cause the adults to remain small. Water quality

Xiphophorus evelynae
Rosen, 1960
Pueblo Platy

Taxonomic Details

First described by Donn E. Rosen (1960) in 'Middle-American poeciliid fishes of the genus *Xiphophorus*' *Bull. Fla St. Mus. Biol. Sci.* **5** (4): 57–242.

ETYMOLOGY This species was named for Mrs Evelyn Gordon who in 1939 was instrumental in collecting the first known specimens.

SYNONYMS *X. variatus evelynae* Rosen, 1960

SPECIES-GROUP 2

TYPE LOCALITY Rio Xanthophyll where it meets the Rio Necaxa at Tepexic, Mexico. The type series was collected by M. and E. Gordon on 6 April 1939. The holotype is a male 33 mm SL and the allotype is an adult female 36.3 mm SL. This species is concentrated above a series of cataracts near the village of Necaxa, which is also known as La Mesa. This area is approximately 1,220 m above sea level. At one time the waters of the Rio Necaxa cascaded down into a gorge some 336 m below the plateau, but this area has since been dammed and a reservoir created which feeds a hydro-electric plant. In 1939 this species was collected in the pools and river below the falls and it was here that the largest and most strongly-marked fish were found. In some males the dorsal fin was so extended that it reached back almost to the caudal peduncle. However, a severe hurricane in 1940 flooded this area, creating currents which very few fish would have been able to survive, and, when this area was collected again in 1957, no *X. evelynae* could be found, despite other species of

Xiphophorus evelynae. Male from Rio Necaxa, Puebla State, Mexico.

livebearers having re-established themselves. It is possible that the water
being diverted through the hydro-
electric plant would make re-stocking
from above impossible.

Distribution
Mexico: So far, this species has been
found only in the Rio Tecolutla system
in Puebla.

Description
This species has a body form somewhat
similar to the better-known *X. variatus*
platy, to which it is quite closely
related. The female is rather drab in
colour, being brownish across the
back with a whitish stomach area.
Sometimes she will have fine black
spots across the back and rear of the
body. The underlying coloration of
the male is similar. However, it is
overlaid with a purple sheen and lots
of fine spots particularly concentrated
towards the rear of the fish. From just
behind the pectoral fin to behind the
dorsal fin, there is a region of vertical
black bars which appear on the dominant males of the colony when they are
courting. The male's caudal and dorsal
fins are yellow to bright orange whilst
the female's are pale yellow to clear.
Altogether, this is an attractive species
which deserves more attention in the
specialist hobby than it currently
receives.

SIZE Males: 40 mm. Females: 50 mm.

Temperament, Care and Breeding
This is a peaceful adaptable fish which
does well in the aquarium. It will
colony-breed without too much difficulty once the adults are used to
being with small fry, but big old
females will sometimes turn cannibal-
istic and attack new-born babies. Large
males will often spar in the centre of
the tank, at which time the colours can
be truly breathtaking.

Broods are born on a 4-weekly cycle
and can number up to 50 robust fry.
The new-born babies will hide in the
plants at the bottom of the tank for the
first few days, after which they venture
out in search of food.

This species was first imported to
the UK in April 1979 by Howard
Preston, who had met Dr Radda in
Puebla, Mexico, and was given some
of his wild-caught specimens. No
information was given about the collection point at that time.

Xiphophorus gordoni
Miller & Minckley, 1963
Cuartro Cienegas Platy

Taxonomic Details
First described by Robert Rush Miller
and W. L. Minckley (1963) in '*Xiphophorus gordoni*, a new species of
platyfish from Coahuila, Mexico'
Copeia **1963** (3): 538–46.

ETYMOLOGY This species was named
for Dr Myron Gordon who did so
much work on this genus and greatly
extended our understanding of platies
and swordtails.

SYNONYMS None

SPECIES-GROUP 1

TYPE LOCALITY Laguna Santa Tecla,
32 km by air, south-southeast of the
town of Cuartro Cienegas, in the state
of Coahuila, Mexico. The types were
collected by R. R. Miller, C. L. Hubbs,
W. L. Minckley, D. R. Tindall and
José Lugo Jr on 9 April 1961. The
holotype is a 24 mm SL male and the
allotype is a 24.6 mm SL female.

Distribution
Mexico: This species occurs in spring-
fed pools and streams heated by volcanic activity in the area around Santa
Tecla in the Cuartro Cienegas basin. It

Xiphophorus gordoni. Male from Santa Tecla, Cuartro Cienegas Basin, Coahuila State, Mexico.

is most commonly found in a spring-fed ditch entering the *laguna* and in the vegetation-choked, silt-bottomed, marshy areas adjacent to the outlet of the *laguna*, also possibly in the original stream, which has been mostly modified into a canal called La Polilla. The original stream drained the eastern side of the basin.

Description
The Cuartro Cienegas Platy, in common with other members of this species-group, has a strongly bi-coloured body, being brown on the back and off-white on the belly. The 2 colour regions are separated by a dark, zigzag, mid-lateral stripe running from just behind the eye to the caudal peduncle. Both sexes have a gravid spot when mature. All the fins are brownish with the dorsal having 2 darker crescents in it. The bottom ray of the male's caudal fin is black and

the body has a very attractive bluish sheen when in good condition.

SIZE Males: 30 mm. Females: 40 mm.

Temperament, Care and Breeding
This is a shy, retiring species which does best in a well-planted aquarium with plenty of hiding places. In nature, this species comes from warm-water springs and streams which have an average temperature of 34°C. However, the aquarium stocks have now adjusted to cooler temperatures of approximately 26°C. Broods are born on a monthly cycle and normally number about 20. The females tend to be short-lived and usually manage only 3 or 4 broods before becoming too old to breed. Since the new-born fry are often attacked by large adults if they are not heavily fed with live food, it is best to isolate the female when she is about to give birth.

Xiphophorus helleri
Heckel, 1848
Green Swordtail

Taxonomic Details
First described by J. Heckel (1848) in 'Eine neue Gattung von Poecilien mit rochenartigem Anklammerungs-Organ' *Sitzber. K. Akad. Wiss. Wien, Math. Nat. Cl.* **1**: 289–303.

ETYMOLOGY Named for Herr Heller who first brought this species back to Germany.

SYNONYMS
X. guentheri Jordan & Evermann, 1896
X. jalapae Meek, 1902
X. brevis Regan, 1907
X. strigatus Regan, 1907
X. rachovii Regan, 1911
X. hellerii guntheri Hubbs, 1935
X. h. helleri Del Campo, 1938
X. h. strigatus De Buen, 1940
X. h. brevis Hubbs & Gordon, 1943

SPECIES-GROUP 3

TYPE LOCALITY The small streams and brooks around the town of Orizaba in Veracruz State, Mexico.

Distribution
Mexico: This species has the most extensive natural range of any species of *Xiphophorus*. In the north it extends from, and includes, the Rio Nautla in Veracruz State. It reaches as far south as the independent Atlantic coastal tributaries of north-western Honduras. This represents a straight-line distance of some 1,300 km from the most northerly location to the most southerly. This has been widened considerably in recent decades by accidental introductions around the world. The preferred habitats for this species are flowing streams with a sand, gravel or rocky substrate. In such places, they gather in pools in the stream bed and along the banks, although some individuals will be found scattered in the main streams and in lowland pools and swamps.

Description
This is a very slender species with the body depth being only equal to about one-third of the body length. There is a strong mid-lateral stripe running from the eye to the caudal peduncle. The dorsal fin is long-based and has a straight to slightly convex edge. The lower rays of the caudal fin of the male are elongated to form a sword which, in most wild strains, is equal to the body length. The coloration of this species is extremely variable in the wild, with many populations exhibiting several different morphs as well as being unique from other populations. The following are just a small selection of the various types:

● **Laguna de Catemaco** – In this population the body tends to be somewhat more slender than most other forms and the sword length is greater than the body length. The sword is yellow and edged in black. The dorsal fin lacks any of the red spots commonly seen in other forms and the fins are clear to pale yellow. The body has a black stripe running from the eye to the caudal peduncle and there can be 1 or 2 more faint black lines above this. The body is an iridescent bronze or blue, depending on where within the lake and surrounding streams the fish were collected.

● **Rio Atoyac** – In this population the body form and sword length are standard for this species but the coloration varies tremendously within the population. In some fish the body is plain green whilst in others this coloration is overlaid with black spots. Rare indi-

Xiphophorus helleri. Male from Rio Belize, Belize. This male is of the black-speckled form.

viduals are red. The single mid-lateral stripe is either red or black and the dorsal has rows of red spots on a clear, yellow or red background.

● **Rio Coatzacoalcos** – In the upper reaches of this river, the body form tends to be somewhat deeper than in many populations and the sword somewhat shorter. The mid-lateral stripe is brownish in coloration and a further 1 or 2 faint reddish lines run above and below this. The sword is yellow, edged in black, and the dorsal fin has red spots on a pale yellow background. The general coloration of this population can be very similar to the sympatric Yellow Swordtail (*X. clemenciae*) and it is only the red spots in the caudal peduncle of the yellow sword which is a definitive characteristic. The mid-lateral stripe on the green sword is much darker as well but this can depend on the mood of the fish.

Many other forms of this fish exist and it would be impossible to describe

them all. The man-made colour varieties are described in Chapter 9.

SIZE Males: 80 mm. Females: 100 mm. However, various populations achieve differing sizes in the aquarium.

Temperament, Care and Breeding
This is an easy fish to keep and breed, being at home in a community tank with medium-sized fish. Small fish can be bullied by large males and fighting between males will often break out. They will adapt to most water conditions and will tolerate a wide temperature range. Fry are born every 28 days and can number upwards of 200. These are usually strong, robust babies which grow quickly and reach 5 cm in only 3 months if fed on large amounts of live Brine Shrimps. Large, regular, partial water-changes should be undertaken and a cool temperature of only 22°C should be maintained to raise the fry. This will slow down the onset of sexual maturity and produce larger more robust fish in the end.

This species is notorious for producing broods with skewed sex ratios. Some populations are known to naturally produce many more males than females or vice versa. Many theories have been put forward to account for this but, as yet, no definite answer has been found.

Xiphophorus maculatus
(Gunther, 1866)
Southern Platy

Taxonomic Details
First described by A. Gunther (1866) in *A Catalogue of the Fishes in the British Museum* London, **6**: 368 pp.

ETYMOLOGY The name refers to the black spot patterns so common in this species.

SYNONYMS
Platypoecilus maculatus Gunther, 1866
Poecilia maculata Regan, 1906

SPECIES-GROUP 2

TYPE LOCALITY The type specimens are 2 females, the largest of which is 32 mm SL with a spotted dorsal fin and 1 spot in the caudal peduncle. The other fish is 30 mm SL and has 2 tail-spot patterns: Comet and One Spot. These fish were purchased by the Natural History Museum from Cuming who obtained them from Mr Salle. The collection site was only given as Mexico by Mr Salle who, it is assumed, collected the fish himself.

Distribution
Mexico, Belize, Guatemala: The Southern Platy is another species with a very wide range in the wild. It is found in the Rio Jamapa in Veracruz State, Mexico, along the Atlantic coastal drainages to Belize and Guatemala. It is restricted to the lower elevations and coastal plains, where the temperatures are somewhat warmer. This species has now been introduced to many parts of the world by Man. In nature, it is concentrated in spring pools, ditches and swamps. It can rarely be found in slow-moving streams and main river channels. The substrates are normally mud and clay with dense stands of aquatic plants or emergents. It is rarely found where there is no plant life.

Description
The Southern Platy is a deep-bodied species in which all the fins are rounded. There are many different colour forms in nature. The following are a small selection:

● **Rio Jamapa** – Within this population there are numerous variations. One of the commoner forms has a brown body with a black shoulder-spot and a black flash in the front of the dorsal fin with red behind. Another form has a reddish body whilst another has a black body.
● **Rio Papaloapan** – Once again, there is variation within the population, but one of the best of the black-form males comes from this river system. The body is jet black, the head is brown and the fins are clear with the exception of the dorsal, which has a row of black spots. Unfortunately, fish from this population remain small, with a full-grown male only achieving 25 mm.
● **Rio Belize** – The fish of the Rio Belize population usually have a few black blotches over the body and a reddish sheen. The fins are often clear. However, red pigment patterns are quite common in this region and many different patterns will be found throughout the population. The Red Iris Platy comes from this river. In this form, the iris of the eye and part of the

Xiphophorus maculatus. Female from Rio Jamapa, Veracruz State, Mexico. This population is tremendously variable in the wild.

head are bright red. This is normally exhibited on a pale brown body which makes it even more noticeable than would otherwise be the case.

SIZE Males: 40 mm. Females: 50 mm. However, there is great variation in size depending upon population.

Temperament, Care and Breeding
The Southern Platy is the perfect community fish, being small enough for most community tanks and totally peaceful. It will tolerate a wide range of conditions but prefers warmer temperatures than most of the swordtails, with about 26°C suiting it best. Plenty of plants in the tank makes it feel at home and, if maintained in a species tank, it will flock-breed if well fed. Broods are born on a monthly cycle and can number upwards of 40.

The Southern Platy is unusual in having some populations with 3 sex chromosomes instead of 2. Extensive collecting in the Rios Jamapa and Papaloapan systems of Veracruz State, Mexico, have only produced fish with X and Y chromosomes but, throughout the rest of this species' range, and particularly in the Belize and Guatemalan populations, W sex chromosomes are common. Three of these genotypes (WY, WY and XX) are females and 2 (XY and YY) are males. This means that there are 6 possible matings between the genotypes. Of these, 4 will produce equal sex ratios, 1 will produce 3 females to every male, and the other will produce all males. This rather complicated system may be more widespread within *Xiphophorus* and could be one of the reasons for skewed sex ratios which occur from time to time in many other species and populations of this genus.

Xiphophorus malinche
Rauchenberger, Kallman & Morizot, 1990
Highland Swordtail

Taxonomic Details
First described by Mary Rauchen-berger, Klaus Kallman and Donald C. Morizot (1990) in 'Monophyly and geography of the Rio Panuco Basin swordtails (genus *Xiphophorus*) with descriptions of four new species' *Am. Mus. Novit.* No. 2975: 41 pp.

ETYMOLOGY This species was named for Malinche (Malintzin) who was captured by Hernan Cortes in 1519 and baptized as Marina. Despite being an Indian slave, Dona Marina became Cortes's interpreter, secretary, advisor and mistress.

SYNONYMS None

SPECIES-GROUP 2

CLADE Cortezi

TYPE LOCALITY The holotype is a 46 mm long male collected on 18 February 1988, by K. D. Kallman, D. C. Morizot, M. Rauchenberger and A. Basolo in the Rio Claro at Tlatzintla in the Rio Moctezuma Drainage, Rio Panuco basin, Hidalgo State, Mexico.

Distribution
Mexico: So far, this species has been found in the headwaters of the Rios Moctezuma, Atlapexco and Calabozo drainages of the Rio Panuco basin, at elevations from 650 m up to 1,280 m. At its higher elevations this species has been collected in water as cold as 15°C.

Xiphophorus malinche. Male from Rio Calnali. This fish is one of those bred by Dr Kallman.

Xiphophorus malinche. Female from Rio Calnali. This is one of Dr Kallman's fish.

Description

The Highland Swordtail is, to my mind, the most attractive species in this clade. As with all members of the clade, there is a single zigzag stripe running from the eye to the caudal peduncle. Along the body of both sexes can be seen a series of bars or broken blotches. The sword is shorter than in the Cortes Swordtail and somewhat thicker. In young specimens the sword is often upturned, but this becomes less noticeable as the fish matures. The male has a lemon-yellow dorsal fin but in the Rio Claro collection the caudal fin is also lemon-yellow.

SIZE Males: 50 mm. Females: 50 mm.

Temperament, Care and Breeding

The Highland Swordtail behaves some-what differently in the wild, when compared to other members of this or the *X. montezumae* clade. Normally, mature males of these clades will hide amongst large rocks and dart away when disturbed. This makes collection of mature specimens very difficult. However, in the Highland Swordtail, large numbers of fully-mature fish were collected under floating vegetation in shallow water above a sandy bottom.

Another difference with this species is its distribution. The other members of this clade are, in general, found at lower elevations than the Highland Swordtail.

It was for this reason that the common name was chosen. It would therefore follow that this species will prefer cooler temperatures in the aquarium than might normally be given to swordtails.

Xiphophorus meyeri
Schartl & Shroeder, 1988
Muzquiz Platy

Taxonomic Details
First described by Schartl & Shroeder
(1988) in 'A new species of the genus
Xiphophorus' *Senckenberg. Biol.* **68**:
311–21.

ETYMOLOGY   This species was named
for Herr Manfred K. Meyer. However,
another description of this fish was
published by the Mexican scientists
who discovered the fish in 1982. They
named this species '*X. marmoratus*'
and, although the scientists concerned
(H. Obregon and S. Contreras-
Balderas) had been working on this
fish for many years, the honour of
naming the species goes to the German
scientists who managed to publish
first.

SYNONYMS   *X. marmoratus* Obregon
& Contreras, 1988

SPECIES-GROUP   1

TYPE LOCALITY   Muzquiz, in the state
of Coahuila, Mexico. The type
specimen was collected by E. Hnilicka
on 22 September 1982. It is a 27 mm
SL male.

Distribution
Mexico: This species is known only
from the type locality and closely-
allied headwater springs and ponds.

Description
This is one of the most recently-
described species of *Xiphophorus* and
is an extremely close relative of the
Monterrey Platy (*X. couchianus*). In
body form it is similar to the Monterrey
Platy and has the same strong bi-
coloration, with the back and upper

Xiphophorus meyeri. Male from Muzquiz, Coahuila State, Mexico. This fish is
the descendant of Dr Kallman's stock.

sides dark brown and the belly and lower ventral regions whitish. The male has 2 dark crescents in the dorsal fin and, whilst the female still shows this coloration, it is very much reduced. Both sexes can have heavy black speckling along the flanks, but unspotted individuals occur in the wild. At the present time, the aquarium stock has both forms but, since the black-speckled individuals are so much more attractive than their unspotted brethren, it can only be a question of time before the unspotted morph is lost in the aquarium hobby. Captive stocks of the Monterrey Platy have lost the spotting over the decades of being maintained in the aquarium.

SIZE Males: 30 mm. Females: 40 mm.

Temperament, Care and Breeding

This species has many of the attributes of its close relative, being somewhat touchy about its tank conditions, and is difficult to establish in a new set-up. It is a somewhat more nervous species than the Monterrey Platy and, in general, will not be seen swimming about the aquarium very much at all. It prefers to hide in the corners or amongst the plant cover, which seems to be an absolute must for it to do well. This nervousness will, in all probability, abate as the fish is taken through several generations in the aquarium.

It eats all foods, but will do best if fed on a diet with a very large percentage of live foods as opposed to flake-food. The fry are born on a monthly cycle but this can be a little erratic, with females having a resting period during the winter months. Average brood sizes have so far been about 15 but up to 40 have been known. The fry grow fairly quickly and start to sex out from about the fourth month onwards. Females become reproductive at between 4 and 6 months old.

Xiphophorus milleri
Rosen, 1960
Catemaco Platy

Taxonomic Details
First described by Donn E. Rosen (1960) in 'Middle-American poeciliid fishes of the genus *Xiphophorus*' *Bull. Fla St. Mus. Biol. Sci.* **5** (4): 57–242.

ETYMOLOGY This species was named for Dr Robert Rush Miller who collected this and many other new species of fish.

SYNONYMS None

SPECIES-GROUP 2

TYPE LOCALITY A small tributary of Lake Catemaco about 3.2 km southeast of the town at Catemaco. The holotype is a male 23.2 mm SL and the allotype is a female 28.5 mm SL. Both fish were collected by R. R. Miller and M. Miller on 29 March, 1957, together with 241 young to adult fish.

Distribution
Mexico: This species is known only from Lake Catemaco and its surrounding feeder streams. In general, this species is found in the shallow areas close to the banks of the lake, where there is some growing vegetation, but it is most prolific in the small shallow streams which flow into the lake, where there are considerably more growing plants and hiding places.

Description
Despite its very limited range, this small platy has evolved into a number of different morphs. Three micro-melanophore patterns are known – One Spot, Large One Spot and Striped. This striped pattern is similar to the patterning exhibited by Montezuma Swordtails. Two macromelanophore patterns are known: one consists of

Xiphophorus milleri. Male from Lake Catemaco. Large morph, black stripe, black gonopodium. This is just one of many different forms of this fish.

Xiphophorus milleri. Male from Lake Catemaco. Black small morph.

spots on the body and the other of rows of spots in dusky bands on the flanks. Dr R. R. Miller reports that the flanks and belly of the adult males were deep yellow to orange in late March when he collected them.

The commonest form has a slender body with a brownish-green body coloration fading to white on the belly. The male may exhibit fine black speckling, particularly towards the rear of the body. Where the lateral line meets the tail is a single dark spot. The fins in general are clear, with the dorsal having 2 dusky crescents, one in the mid-region of the fin and the other at the edge. Other morphs include a black form, in which the fine black speckles on the male are intensified so that the fish is almost completely black. Females of this strain usually have several black stripes along the flanks. This seems to be the smallest morph, with males barely reaching 15 mm. The largest morph has black stripes along the body in both sexes and the male may exhibit a false gravid spot and a black gonopodium. Females of this morph, when in good condition, take on a dusky appearance over the ventral regions. Full adult size for males of this strain seems to be about double that of the black form and even the females are larger. Another morph has males with yellow dorsal fins and no doubt there are many more variations in the wild.

SIZE Males: 15–30 mm. Females: 45 mm.

Temperament, Care and Breeding

This is an easy fish to maintain in the aquarium, being at home both in a species tank or a community tank with other small peaceful fish. Whilst good tank conditions are appreciated, this species will stand a certain degree of neglect. Ideally, the temperature should be approximately 23°C but it will tolerate anywhere between 20° and 27°C, with no obvious signs of stress. In simulation of its natural habitat, some plant cover in the tank is appreciated, as it gives the females somewhere to hide from the over-amorous males. The diet should consist of small live foods, such as *Daphnia* and baby Brine Shrimps, but the fish seem to survive on a diet consisting of flake-food alone, if only that is offered. Broods are born on a monthly cycle, with numbers up to 50 being known but about 20 being average. The fry grow fairly quickly and males start to sex out in only 3 months. These early-maturing fish will remain small and carry the genes for small size and early maturation; careful selection of breeding-stock is therefore a must, if the size is to be maintained over the generations. The large-morph strains of this fish are more prone to eating their fry, so it is wise to isolate a gravid female which is ready to give birth. Once the fry are about 1 month old they can be returned to the adult tank. The small morphs can be colony-bred without any problems.

Xiphophorus montezumae
Jordan & Snyder, 1901
Montezuma Swordtail

Taxonomic Details

First described by D. S. Jordan & J. O. Snyder (1901) in 'Notes on a collection of fishes from the rivers of Mexico, with descriptions of twenty new species' *Bull. U.S. Fish. Comm.* **19**: 115–47.

ETYMOLOGY   Named for the Emperor Montezuma.

SYNONYMS   *X. montezumae montezumae* Rosen, 1960

SPECIES-GROUP 3

CLADE Montezumae

TYPE LOCALITY 'Rio Verde', correctly called the Rio Gallinas, near the town of Rascon in the state of San Luis Potosí, Mexico. The holotype is a female collected by J. O. Snyder on 24 January 1899. Adult males were said to be scarce in this collection. This was probably due to the difficulty of catching adult male swordtails rather than any lack of them in the wild population.

Range
Mexico: Found mostly in northern tributaries of the Rio Santa Maria and in the Rio Gallinas system, this species also occurs in Arroyo's La Cienega at Ojo Caliente, Cienega Grande and Tanchanaquito.

Description
The Montezuma Swordtail achieves the largest size of all the known Rio Panuco basin swordtails; in the aquarium, male fish from the Arroyo Cienega Grande easily reach up to 70 mm whilst the females reach 75 mm.

The Montezuma Swordtail is a slender species with multiple zigzag lateral stripes and a sword length equal to the body length on average. The sword length can be anywhere between ¾ and 1½ times the body length. The black spotting on the sides of some fish is only present in the Rio Gallinas population, and then only in some specimens. A few males of all the populations of this species develop a deep bronze to red coloration in the wild. This coloration was noted by J. O. Snyder in the original collection of this species.

The dorsal fin is shorter-based than in the Northern Mountain Swordtail and tends to be more sail-like, particularly in the males. Females lack the sword extension but otherwise are similar. Some males have kinks in their swords; whilst aquarists will no doubt try to breed this out of their fish, it is quite normal in the wild.

Many of the fish shown in the literature as this species are incorrectly named or hybrids.

SIZE Males: 70 mm. Females: 75 mm.

Temperament, Care and Breeding
This species is a peaceful attractive swordtail which does well in a community tank of medium-sized fish. It likes a temperature of about 24°C and a clean, well-planted tank. It eats all foods and enjoys some variation in its diet. Broods are produced on a 28-day cycle with numbers ranging from 15 to 30 for mature females.

If well fed and maintained in a heavily-planted tank, it can be flock-bred. However, to obtain the best growth rate from the fry, a gravid female should be carefully moved to a small spawning tank about a week before she is due to drop. Remove the female to the colony tank after the fry have been born and raise them in the small tank for about a week before putting them in a large rearing-tank. Ideally this should be about 1 m long for 30 fry and 50 per cent water-changes should be carried out weekly. Once the fry reach 25 mm long a power-filter can be added to create a current, which will simulate conditions in most of the habitats where this fish is found in the wild. If fed twice daily on baby Brine Shrimps, with extra feeds of flake-food, the fry will grow very quickly and should reach 25 mm in under 2 months. In good specimens the sword will not develop until the male is nearly fully grown.

In the Arroyo Cienega Grande population the male may be 70 mm long before he sexes out, by which time the fish concerned may be a year

Xiphophorus montezumae. Male from Rio Gallinas by the town of Tamasopo. The extremely long sword of this species is clearly seen in this specimen.

Xiphophorus montezumae. Female from Rio Gallinas by the town of Tamasopo. The similarity between females of this species and *X. continens* is very obvious.

old. Since, at this stage, most of the females will have reached sexual maturity and produced fry fathered by one of the other males in the tank, it would be easy to confuse this late-sexing-out male with a 'female which has changed sex'. Indeed most, if not all, stories of female swordtails becoming males can be attributed to late-sexing-out males.

Xiphophorus multilineatus
Rauchenberger, Kallman & Morizot, 1990
High-backed Pygmy Swordtail

Taxonomic Details
First described by Mary Rauchen-berger, Klaus Kallman and Donald C. Morizot (1990) in 'Monophyly and geography of the Rio Panuco basic swordtails (genus *Xiphophorus*) with descriptions of four new species' *Am. Mus. Novit.* No. 2975: 41 pp.

ETYMOLOGY This species was named for the many vertical bars which are a distinctive characteristic of this species.

SYNONYMS   *X. nigrensis* Rosen, 1979

SPECIES-GROUP   3

CLADE   *Pygmaeus*

TYPE LOCALITY   The holotype is a small-morph male 2.5 cm long collected on 17 February 1979 by K. D. Kallman, D. C. Morizot, V. Borkoski and G. Peters in the Rio Choy close to where it meets the Rio Tampaon in the Rio Panuco basin in the state of San Luis Potosí, Mexico.

Distribution
Mexico: This species is known only from the Rio Choy system, Rio Panuco drainage, San Luis Potosí State.

Description
Here we have one of the real problem species of swordtail to describe. Many species of *Xiphophorus* contain fish which differ in size as adults, but in this species these differences are very complex and have a tremendous effect on the overall appearance of the fish.

Females and immature males have a single dense mid-lateral stripe formed of zigzags so close together that they appear as a solid line. This runs from the eye to the caudal peduncle and is a characteristic of all species in the Pygmaeus clade. It is present at birth and is bordered above by an area clear of any pigmentation. Both sexes have 2 black crescents in the dorsal fin (although faintly shown in the female), one approximately one-third of the way along the fin and the other at its outermost edge. All other fins are clear except for the male's caudal margin and black-edged sword. The sword is often upcurved, particularly when the male is small.

Males come in 4 size-morphs. All sizes have an iridescent blue sheen over the flanks but in larger-morph males, many vertical bars will be seen as well. In all sizes, except the very smallest morph, there is a black spot at the base of the pectoral fin. In the caudal peduncle there is a black, vertical mark, which is much better developed in the larger morphs than in the smaller. Sword length varies tremendously between the different size morphs. In the small morph the sword may be as small as 1–2 mm and the overall body size of a mature fish will only be 25 mm. However, at the other extreme, we have males of up to 40 mm body length, with swords equal in length to their bodies. Gold-morph males also occur but these, so far, have only been found in the short-sword form. Body depth is greater in the large morph, and the common

Xiphophorus multilineatus. Long-sword form male from the Rio Choy. This fish is a descendant of Dr Kallman's stock.

Xiphophorus multilineatus. Short-sword male from the Rio Choy. The differences between the short-sword and long-sword forms of this species are very marked.

name of High-backed Pygmy Sword-tail comes from the almost hump-backed appearance of these males. The other 2 size morphs cover the intermediate range. Here we have a situation where the 2 extreme forms of a single species can look like 2 totally different species. A similar situation occurs in only 1 other swordtail species and that is *X. nigrensis*. It has been postulated that the other member of the clade (*X. pygmaeus*), as well as the fish we see today, used to have a long-sworded large morph but this was lost due to some environmental factor, such as heavy predation on these more conspicuous fish.

SIZE   Males: 25–40 mm. Females: 40 mm.

Temperament, Care and Breeding

This is one of the real problem species of the *Xiphophorus* world. To be at its best, it needs to be housed in a large, well-planted tank with filtration, aera-tion and regular, partial water-changes. It is a timid species, which spends most of its time hidden amongst the foliage, only dashing out occasionally to grab some food. All foods are taken, but the emphasis should be on live foods.

Small-morph males start to sex out in only 3 months and, if they are allowed to, will take over the colony. The large-morph males may take up to 8 months to sex out, by which time the females are often too old to breed successfully. Hence, multi-generational colonies are essential if the large morph is to be maintained and, if the foundation stock of this colony includes some small-morph fish, very careful monitoring will have to take place if the large morph is not to be lost from the gene pool.

In the wild, large-morph males tend to spend much of their time in the open water where the current is strongest, whilst small-morph males are more often found close to the banks and hidden amongst the plants. These small-morph males use opportunist mating tactics, rushing in to mate with a female with little or no courtship. However, the large-morph males court the females and obtain her active participation in the mating process.

Broods are born on a monthly cycle, but are small in number; about 20 is the maximum, but 5–10 the average. The fry are large at birth and will not be harmed provided that the parents are well fed.

Xiphophorus nezahualcoyotl
Rauchenberger, Kallman & Morizot, 1990
Northern Mountain Swordtail

Taxonomic Details

First described by Mary Rauchen-berger, Klaus Kallman and Donald C. Morizot (1990) in 'Monophyly and geography of the Rio Panuco basin swordtails (genus *Xiphophorus*) with descriptions of four new species' *Am. Mus. Novit.* No. 2975: 41 pp.

ETYMOLOGY   In an effort to move away from the sycophantic habit of naming fish after each other that many ichthy-ologists have slipped into, Rauchen-berger *et al.* decided to name many of their new species after Indians who had played a major part in Mexican history. Since the Montezuma Sword-tail was named in honour of Monte-zuma, who was a monarch of the Aztecs in the Aztec Triple Alliance, it was felt that its sister species should be named for Nezahualcoyotl, the poet–philosopher Emperor of Tezcoco

Xiphophorus nezahualcoyotl. Male from Rio Santa Maria de Guadalupe. This is a descendant of Dr Kallman's stock.

(Texcoco) who was his equal in status and power. The problem with this wonderful idea is that nobody can pronounce such a mouthful.

SYNONYMS

X. montezumae montezumae Rosen, 1960

X. montezumae (Hamburg, 1964), Lechner & Radda, 1987

Xiphophorus sp. nov. Zimmer & Kallman, 1988

SPECIES-GROUP 3

CLADE Montezumae

TYPE LOCALITY The holotype is a male 43 mm long and was collected by K. D. Kallman, D. C. Morizot, and M. Ryan in the Arroyo Gallitos 0.5 km west of Gallitos, in the state of Tampico, Mexico.

Distribution

Mexico: This species is found in the Rio el Salto, Rio Tamesi drainage, Rio Santa Maria de Guadalupe, Rio los Gatos and Rio Tanchachin and also in the extreme headwaters of Rio Sabinas and Arroyo el Zarco. It is usually found in flowing streams and rivers with a strong current. Normally, there are few or no submerged aquatic plants and only small stands of emergent plants. The substrates are normally sand, gravel or rocks. Very rarely are these fish found over a mud or clay bottom.

Description

In common with the Montezuma Swordtail, the Northern Mountain Swordtail has multiple zigzag stripes along the body but a much shorter sword index averaging just over half of the body length. Apart from the shorter sword length, the body is also deeper, giving this species an altogether more robust appearance. The dorsal fin is longer-based and the sword is more distinctly upturned, particularly in smaller males.

This species is somewhat smaller than the Montezuma Swordtail, being fully grown at 50 mm for the male and 55 mm for the female. Coloration differs between individual fish. In better-coloured specimens, the black spotting across the flanks of the male is profuse and the sword is yellow-orange edged in black.

SIZE Males: 50 mm. Females: 55 mm.

Temperament, Care and Breeding
Aquarium maintenance for this species is much the same as for the Montezuma Swordtail although, as it occurs at lower altitudes, slightly warmer temperatures are appreciated, with an average of about 25°C being ideal. Higher temperatures will make the fish grow more quickly, but they will sex out sooner, so the final adult size will be smaller than the final adult size in fish which have been reared at lower temperatures. Being a somewhat smaller species, males tend to sex out at a younger age than the Montezuma Swordtail.

Broods are produced on a monthly cycle, with older females becoming a little erratic at times in their cycle. Sometimes an old female will not produce any fry for several months, then she will produce a bumper brood, after which she dies. Brood numbers are on average 25 but as many as 50 have been reported.

Xiphophorus nigrensis
Rosen, 1960
El Abra Pygmy Swordtail

Taxonomic Details
First described by Donn E. Rosen (1960) in 'Middle-American poeciliid fishes of the genus *Xiphophorus*' *Bull. Fla St. Mus. Biol. Sci.* **5** (4): 57–242.

ETYMOLOGY The scientific name is derived from the Latin *niger* = 'black' and *ensis* = 'sword' and refers to the black ventral margin of the caudal appendage of adult males. The common name of El Abra Pygmy Swordtail comes from the diminutive size of this species and the mountain (El Abra) out of which flows the only river in which this species lives.

SYNONYMS *X. pygmaeus nigrensis* Rosen, 1960

SPECIES-GROUP 3

CLADE Pygmaeus

TYPE LOCALITY *Nacimiento* del Rio Choy, 4 km north of Hotel Taninul, 3 km north of road (Route 110, Valles-Tampico), in the state of San Luis Potosí, Mexico. The holotype is a male 29 mm SL which was collected by D. E. Rosen, M. S. Gordon and M. Gordon on 19 January 1957.

Distribution
Mexico: This species is known only from a northern tributary of the Rio Tampaon. This is most commonly known as the Rio Choy but, at the entrance to the cave out of which this river swiftly flows, the river is also known as the Rio Florido. This species is found throughout the whole of the length of this tributary but it is commonest near the cave mouth, where the water is clear and the current is fast-flowing. Downstream, the water tends

to become somewhat slower-moving with dense plant growth, especially towards the banks.

Description

This species is relatively slender in shape, although not as slim as *X. pygmaeus*. Females have the single, longitudinal, mid-lateral stripe of all the pygmy swords and a basic body coloration of greyish blue. The dorsal fin of both sexes has 2 crescents: one close to the body and the other forming a dark edge to the fin. However, this coloration is very faint in the female. All the other fins are clear, except the male's sword which is usually black-edged and can have a yellow interior. The body coloration of a fully mature male is an intense steel blue and the

mid-lateral stripe will fade out. Three size morphs of the males have been identified in this species, with the largest having a sword almost equal to its body length, whilst the smallest morph may have no caudal appendage at all! The sword on this species is usually upcurved and on the long-sword morph will equal the body length. The long-sword morph will also have a proportionally deeper body than the smaller morph.

SIZE   Males: 25–40 mm. Females: 40 mm.

Temperament, Care and Breeding

This has proven to be the most difficult of all the swordtails to adapt to aquarium conditions. It is very sensitive to

Xiphophorus nigrensis. Two males from the Rio Choy population. The upper fish is a young male of the long-sword form, just sexing out at 6 months of age. The lower fish is a young male of the short-sword form, just sexing out at 3 months of age. Both fish are fully grown in body size but the sword will reach a length equal to the body length in the long-sworded form.

water conditions and susceptible to parasitic infestation. The tank should be well planted with filtration, aeration and regular, small, partial water-changes. Large shifts in pH can very easily cause distress or death in this species. The adults are very shy but, when maintained in a multi-generational colony situation, will show themselves more often. They eat all foods but have a preference for live and frozen, with flake-food being tolerated. Broods are born on a monthly cycle and females are fertile from about the third month through to about the eight month. Brood sizes are small, 10 being the average but as few as 2 being known from small females and a maximum of 20 for a larger female. Large-morph males sex out from about the fifth month onwards and, if the colony is not carefully controlled, the small-morph males will take over and the large morph will be lost from the genetic pool. The size is controlled by a sex-linked gene, so females are all identical with regard to this factor.

Xiphophorus 'PMH'
Southern Swordtail

Taxonomic Details
This form is discussed by Rosen, D. E. (1979) in 'Fishes from the uplands and intermontane basins of Guatemala: Revisionary studies and comparative geography' *Bull. Am. Mus. Nat. Hist.* **162**, Art. 5: 332–74. However, it has not yet been described as a species in its own right.

SPECIES-GROUP 3

TYPE LOCALITY Not designated as yet.

Distribution
Guatemala: This species is found in the Rio Polochic, Lake Izabal, Bania de Amatique and Rio Motagua drainages. Honduras: Rio Chamelecon, Gulf of Honduras and Rio Lancetilla drainages.

The full range of this form has yet to be discovered but it seems to be limited to the extreme south of the natural range of *Xiphophorus* species.

Description
The Southern Swordtail has many of the attributes of its close relative the Green Swordtail. However, the body tends to be deeper, with a thicker caudal peduncle than many populations of the Green Swordtail. The sword can be equal to the body length when fully mature and is a pale creamy yellow, edged in black. The dorsal fin has rows of red spots, whilst all other fins are clear. The background coloration is an iridescent greenish blue, with 4 red lines running the full length of the body. The brightest and most distinct line runs from the eye to the top of the sword, with the line 1 scale row up being the next most distinctive. The 2 outer red lines are paler and fade when the fish has been disturbed or is not in peak condition.

The red lines on the flanks of this species bear a similarity to those of the Yellow Swordtail (*X. clemenciae*). However, the sword in the latter species is a clear lemon-yellow colour. The distinctive red spots in the Yellow Swordtail are clearly defined and, whilst the lines of the Southern Swordtail tend to break up into red zigzag marks in the caudal peduncle, the differences are still great enough to separate the 2 species on coloration alone.

SIZE Males: 50 mm. Females: 60 mm. However, in the aquarium this species has been known to achieve up to 125

Xiphophorus 'PMH'. Male from the Laguna Izabal, Guatemala.

mm SL, which is greater even than the common Green Swordtail.

Temperament, Care and Breeding

In common with its close relative the Green Swordtail, the Southern Swordtail is reported as living in a wide range of habitats from swamp ponds and small streams to rivers with strong currents.

This is a large, robust swordtail which has done well in the aquarium. It prefers large well-planted aquaria with filtration and aeration or, better still, a small tropical pond maintained at temperatures between 19° and 21°C. Under such conditions this fish will grow to an enormous size and the body depth will be markedly greater than when maintained in a small aquarium or at high temperatures.

Broods are born on a monthly cycle, although cool water conditions will extend this to 5 weeks rather than 4. A large adult female may be expected to drop several hundred young but even a young 50 mm female may produce up to 80 fry. These are large and well formed at birth and will grow very quickly if given large quarters and plenty of baby Brine Shrimps.

The best males may be over a year old before they sex out and anything up to 2 years old before they achieve their full sword development. One problem with this species has been skewed sex ratios.

Out of over 250 young bred and reared by us from 2 females, no female was ever produced. Such skewed sex ratios are well known amongst both cultivated and wild forms of the Green Swordtail, Comma Swordtail and Upland Swordtail but it makes the long-term maintenance of this species a major problem.

Xiphophorus pygmaeus
Hubbs & Gordon, 1963
Slender Pygmy Swordtail

Taxonomic Details
First described by C. L. Hubbs and M. Gordon (1943) in 'Studies of cyprinodont fishes. 19. *Xiphophorus pygmaeus*, new species from Mexico' *Copeia* **1943** (1): 31–3.

ETYMOLOGY Named for its diminutive size. Due to increasing numbers of common names for this fish and its relatives, Rauchenberger *et al.* proposed new common names for all the Rio Panuco basin swordtails and we have used these in preference to others which have appeared in the aquatic literature before.

SYNONYMS *X. pygmaeus pygmaeus* Rosen, 1960

SPECIES-GROUP 3

CLADE Pygmaeus

TYPE LOCALITY The Rio Axtla in the state of San Luis Potosí, Mexico. The holotype is a 25 mm SL male collected by Myron Gordon and Salvador Coronado on 14 April 1939, together with 173 paratypes 14–32 mm long, including 16 adult males. In this collection some gold-morph males were noted.

Distribution
Mexico: This species is very common throughout the Rio Huichihuayan and can also be found in the lower 6 km of the Rio Tancuilin, before it joins the Rio Axtla, and from here to about half-way towards the Rio Moctezuma. Surprisingly, it has not been found in any other tributaries of the Rio Axtla system. Since Gordon, in 1953, reported that this species prefers a steep slope below overhanging banks, this information has regularly been repeated without even being confirmed. However, Dr Kallman reports that this species is much more commonly found in regions of heavy plant growth, which would tie in with the preferred habitats of the other short-sworded *Xiphophorus*.

Description
The Slender Pygmy Swordtail, as the common name would suggest, is a small, very slender species. It has a single mid-lateral stripe, extending from the mouth through the eye to the caudal peduncle. This is made up of numerous zigzag lines which are so densely packed as to give the appearance of a single unbroken line. The basic body colour is brown on the back with the edge of each scale darker giving a net-like appearance. Below the mid-lateral stripe the body is whitish with a hint of a blue sheen (this morph is sometimes known as the Blue Pygmaeus, but this common name has more to do with wishful thinking than real coloration!). Females have a gravid spot and here the blue sheen is much more intense. The dorsal fin is short both in height and base length and has 2 dusky crescents, the first about one-third of the way up the fin and the other forming a dark edge to the fin. These crescents are much fainter on the female than on the male.

The lower few caudal fin rays of the male are slightly extended to form a very short 'sword' of about 2 mm length although, occasionally, males with swords up to 8 mm have been encountered. Gold-morph males are known in the wild and this strain has been fixed in the hobby. In fully-mature fish the males will be an intense orange-gold throughout the body and fins. Unfortunately, this is controlled by a sex-linked gene on

Xiphophorus pygmaeus. Pair from Rio Huichihuayan. This is the gold form of this species. The males of the normal form have a body colour similar to the female.

the Y chromosome, so only males exhibit this very beautiful coloration. In this species a large-morph male occurs which reaches approximately 30 mm SL whilst the normal form only achieves 25 mm SL.

SIZE Males: 25–30 mm. Females: 40 mm.

Temperament, Care and Breeding
This is a shy, retiring species which likes plenty of plant cover in the tank to feel secure. If almost any other species is placed in the tank with it, the Slender Pygmy Swordtail will go into decline and fade away. For many

years this was considered a real problem fish and very few people had any success with it. However, many aquarists were using Dr Gordon's description of its natural habitat (i.e. fast-flowing water and no plant life) as a basis for how to house this fish for best results. In fact it seems this species much prefers areas of still waters and heavy plant growth in the wild and this situation should be re-created in the aquaria for best results. Greatest success has been achieved when it has been housed in a 45 l aquarium, at a temperature of 23°C, with lots of Java Moss on the bottom. No filtration was used but regular, partial water-changes were undertaken. The diet consisted of baby Brine Shrimps and an occasional feed of flake-food. Under such conditions, the females reproduced on a monthly cycle and, whilst they had only 6–10 fry, these were not molested and the colony soon grew to quite large numbers. The babies are sexable in about 3 months, at which time the females develop a gravid spot but the males do not. Using this method, this once very rare and difficult aquarium fish has become quite common in the UK specialist-livebearer hobby.

Xiphophorus signum
Rosen & Kallman, 1969
Comma Swordtail

Taxonomic Details
First described by Donn Eric Rosen and Klaus D. Kallman in 'A new fish of the genus *Xiphophorus* from Guatemala, with remarks on the taxonomy of endemic forms' *Am. Mus. Novit.* No. 2379: 29 pp.

ETYMOLOGY Both the scientific name and the common name come from the black mark near the base of the lower caudal fin rays; *signum* in Latin = 'mark, token or sign' and the black blotch looks something like a comma on the caudal fin of juveniles and females. In adult males this mark extends to the top of the sword, which has a thick, deep, black edge to it, and so becomes lost as a distinctive characteristic; however, it is still present.

SYNONYMS *X. helleri signum* Rosen & Kallman, 1969

SPECIES-GROUP 3

TYPE LOCALITY Rio Semococh 15 km south of the town of Sebol, Alta Verapaz, Guatemala. This is a tributary of the Rio Chajmaic, a headwater source of the Rio de la Pasion in the Rio Usumacinta basin. The holotype is an adult male 63.2 mm SL. A total of 413 paratypes, from juveniles to adults (10–70 mm SL) were collected at the same time by using Rotenone.

Distribution
Guatemala: So far, this species has been found only in the Chajmaic valley.

Description
The Comma Swordtail is similar in body form to the Green Swordtail. However, the adult male Comma Swordtail has a sword of only approximately one-third to one-half of its body length whilst the Green Swordtail has a sword approximately equal to its body length. The overall body coloration is pale greenish with a dusky-brown stripe running from behind the eye to the caudal peduncle, where it joins the top of the black mark near the base of the lower caudal fin rays. The dorsal fin is unusual in possessing rays towards the front of the fin which are longer than the rays towards the rear; this gives it a triangular appearance. There are 2 very faint dusky bars in the dorsal, one close to the body and the other at the edge. Occasionally, the fins have a slight yellow flush to them, but this is more noticeable on wild-caught fish than on tank-raised specimens. Males do not have a false gravid spot.

SIZE Males: 75 mm. Females: 100 mm.

Temperament, Care and Breeding
This species is similar in temperament to the Green Swordtail, spending most of its time at the front of the aquarium looking for food. However, it can be a little nervous and will often jump if it

Xiphophorus signum. Male from Rio Chajmaic, Guatemala.

is frightened. For this reason, a close-fitting cover-glass is advisable. It mixes well with other fish of a similar size or smaller and, even though adult males will spar, little damage is usually done to any of the participants.

The Comma Swordtail seems to prefer a temperature of approximately 24°C and a clean aquarium with some plant cover. They often do best if a power-filter is added to the tank to create some current for them to fight against. Gravid females will retire to a quiet corner of the tank to have their babies. These can number several hundred from a large female and the fry are comparable to Green Swordtail babies in size. When born, they do not exhibit the distinctive comma mark, which only develops when the fish reach about 10 mm long.

In this species of swordtail the biggest males can take up to 2 years to sex out. However, females will usually show the gravid spot by the time they are 6 months old and will produce fry at this time, if a fully-mature male is available to mate with. When reared in hard alkaline water, skewed sex ratios have been noted with males outnumbering females by as much as 5 to 1. Whether this is just coincidence or due to some environmental factor has not been established as yet.

Xiphophorus variatus
(Meek, 1904)
Variable Platy

Taxonomic Details
First described by S. E. Meek (1904) in 'The fresh water fishes from Mexico north of the Isthmus of Tehuantepic' *Field Columbian Mus. Publ., Zool. Ser.* **5**: 1–252.

ETYMOLOGY The scientific name refers to the variable coloration of this species in nature.

SYNONYMS *Platypoecilus variatus* Meek, 1904

SPECIES-GROUP 2

TYPE LOCALITY Cuadad Valles in the state of San Luis Potosí, Mexico.

Distribution
Mexico: Found on the Atlantic slope of eastern Mexico from the Rio Sota la Marina system in Tamaulipas State, to the Rio Nautla system in Veracruz State. This species is generally found in spring pools, ditches and swamps, and occasionally in sluggish and rapid-flowing streams. In these habitats there is usually dense aquatic plant growth and many emergents near the banks. The substrate is usually mud and clay.

Description
As its name would suggest, this is a very variable species, with lots of different colour forms throughout its range. The body shape is much more slender than that of the Southern Platy. The dorsal fin has a broader

Xiphophorus variatus. Male from the Rio Choy. Many wild populations of Variable and Southern Platies are small nondescript fish.

base, with generally more rays in it and a straighter edge making the fin look more like a parallelogram in shape. Almost every population is different in colour and great variation occurs even within a population. The following are some of those established within the aquarium:

● **Rio Axtla** – This population has some of the most attractive wild males of this species. In highly-coloured fish, the body has many dark-black zigzag stripes along the flanks. The caudal fin can be bright scarlet and the dorsal fin lemon-yellow; alternatively the fins may be clear or with just a few dusky crescents. In some specimens the body will be iridescent blue overlaid with a few black zigzag stripes and black spots, whilst in others the body may be brown with a Two-spot or One-spot pattern in the caudal peduncle.

● **Rio Mante** – In most specimens of this population the body coloration is brown becoming white on the belly, with the Twin-spot pattern in the caudal peduncle. The males often show a false gravid spot and some vertical bars along the sides.

● **Rio Nautla** – In this population the body coloration is usually brown overlaid with a blue sheen on the males. There are a number of horizontal zigzag lines along the body and a dark blotch in the caudal peduncle. Occasionally, males may have black stripes or spots along the flanks of the body. The dorsal fin of the male is often larger than in most populations of this species.

SIZE Males: 45 mm. Females: 55 mm.

Temperament, Care and Breeding
The Variable Platy has been a staple in the aquatic hobby since it was first introduced to German aquaria in 1931. These were young fish collected by Conrad from a cattle-hole near Tampico.

This is an easily-maintained and easily-bred species which will tolerate poor conditions and is peaceful with other fish. In fact, it admirably fulfils all the criteria which make a fish suitable for community aquarium life. However, to be seen at its best, it needs good tank conditions and plenty of good food. It will tolerate a wide temperature range, and is often collected in small pools where daytime water temperatures may soar to above 30°C whilst night-time temperatures may drop as low as 20°C.

Broods are born on a monthly basis and may number up to 100. These grow fairly slowly and it may be 18 months to 2 years before the males exhibit their full adult coloration, although they are often sexually mature long before this.

Xiphophorus xiphidium
(Gordon, 1932)
Spiketail Platy

Taxonomic Details
First described by Myron Gordon (1932) in 'Dr Myron Gordon going on expedition' *Aquatic Life* **15**: 287–8.

ETYMOLOGY The scientific name *Xiphidium* = 'sword-bearing' and refers to the small spike which mature males of this species exhibit.

SYNONYMS
Platypoecilus variatus Meek, 1904
P. maculatus Regan, 1913
P. xiphidium Gordon, 1932
X. variatus xiphidium Rosen, 1960

SPECIES-GROUP 2

Xiphophorus xiphidium. Two-spot form male from the Rio Purification. On some specimens the entire middle of the fish becomes purple and black but this varies with mood and water conditions.

Xiphophorus xiphidium. One-spot form male from Santa Engracia. This form seems some what larger and more robust than the Rio Purification population but this may be because the Rio Purification strain has been aquarium-bred for many years.

TYPE LOCALITY Though this species was well known for many years, no holotype was ever designated. Therefore the name rests on a syntypic series. In 1960 Rosen designated a lectotype from this series which is a 29 mm SL adult male. This series was collected by Gordon, Creaser and Ostos on 25 April 1930 from the Rio Corona (Rio Santa Engracia) at La Corona, 15 km north of Ciudad Victoria, Rio Santa La Marina System, in the state of Tamaulipas, Mexico.

Distribution
Mexico: This species is found throughout the Rio Sota la Marina system and in ponds and irrigation ditches close to this river system.

Description
This is a deep-bodied species with a high back and short stubby body. The basic body coloration is greenish brown on the top, becoming white on the belly. The fins are pale yellow to clear with a dusky crescent in the dorsal fin of both sexes. The caudal peduncle has one of several tail-spot patterns; One Spot, Two Spot and Crescent are known but others may occur. These have often been associated with certain populations but, in fact, fish with all these tail-spot patterns can be caught in the same net in the wild. As the fish become sexually mature the males will start to develop their full coloration. This seems to be quite variable and well-coloured specimens will have their basic body color overlaid with purple and a number of vertical black bars along the upper flanks ('Parr markings'). Sometimes black spots will also develop and may become so profuse that the whole of the middle region of the fish will be purple with a black saddle. The caudal fin of the male has a short 'sword' but this fish is unequivocally a platy from a scientific point of view. All in all, this is a very attractive fish which deserves a place in the mainstream hobby as opposed to just being maintained by specialist-livebearer enthusiasts.

SIZE Males: 30 mm. Females: 40 mm.

Temperament, Care and Breeding
The Spiketail Platy is not as easy to maintain in the aquarium as the cultivated varieties but it is still a relatively hardy fish. It does best in a well-planted aquarium with regular partial water-changes and a diet which includes some live food. The temperature should be approximately 23°C. Broods are born on a monthly cycle and have been known to number up to 84; however, 20 is a more usual number for a young female and about 35 for a fully-adult fish. This is a relatively short-lived species, so broods need to be saved from young females if the species is to be maintained in the long term. Provided it is well fed and given plenty of low cover, this species will flock-breed.

References and Further Reading

Alvarez, J. (1959) In 'Nuevas especies de *Xiphophorus* e *Hyporhamphus* procedents del Rio Coatzacoalcos' *Cienc. Mex.* **19**: 69–73.

Chambers, J. (1987) 'The cyprinodontiform gonopodium, with an atlas of the gonopodia of the fishes of the genus *Limia*' *J. Fish. Biol.* **30**: 389–418.

Contreras-B., S. & Escalante-C., M. A. (1984) 'Distribution and known impacts of exotic fishes in Mexico' In Courtney, W. R. Jr & Stauffer, J. R. Jr (eds) *Distribution, Biology and Management of Exotic Fishes* John Hopkins University Press, Baltimore, MD, USA: pp. 102–30.

Dawes, J. A. (1991) *Livebearing Fishes. A Guide to their Aquarium Care, Biology and Classification* Blandford Press.

Girard, C. (1859) 'Ichthyological notices, 41–59' *Proc. Acad. Nat. Sci. Philad.* No. 11: 113–22.

Gordon, M. (1928) 'Pigment inheritance in the Mexican killifish. Interaction of factors in *Platypoecilius maculatus*' *J. Hered.* **19** (12): 551–56.

Gordon, M. (1932) 'Dr Myron Gordon going on expedition' *Aquatic Life* **15**: 287–88.

Gordon, M. (1934) 'A history of the common platyfish in aquaria from the earliest times' *Fish Culturist* **14**: 79–92.

Gordon, M. (1953) 'The ecological niche of the pygmy swordtail *Xiphophorus pygmaeus*' *Copeia* **1953** (3): 148–50.

Gordon, M. & Axelrod, H. R. (1968) *Swordtails for the Advanced Hobbyist* T. F. H. Inc.

Gunther, A. (1866) *A Catalogue of the Fishes in the British Museum* London, Vol. **6**: 386 pp.

Heckel, J. (1848) 'Eine neue Gattung von Poecilien mit rochenartigem Anklammerungs-Organ' *Sitzber. K. Akad. Wiss. Wien, Math. Nat. Cl.* **1**: 289–303.

Hubbs, C. L. & Gordon, M. (1943) 'Studies of cyprinodont fishes. 19. *Xiphophorus pygmaeus*, new species from Mexico' *Copeia* **1953** (1): 31–3.

Jacobs, K. (1973) *Livebearing Aquarium Fishes – A Handbook for the Aquarist* T. F. H. Inc.

Jordan, D. S. & Snyder, J. O. (1901) 'Notes on a collection of fishes from the rivers of Mexico, with descriptions of twenty new species' *Bull. U.S. Fish. Comm.* **19**: 115–47.

Kallman, K. D. (n.d.) *Enjoy your Platys and Swordtails* The Pet Library Ltd.

Kallman, K. D. (1970) 'Moon of a million faces' *Trop. Fish World* **1970** (Sept./ Oct.).

Kallman, K. D. (1989) 'Genetic control of size at maturity in *Xiphophorus*' In Meffe, G. K. & Snelson, F. S. Jr (eds) *Ecology and Evolution of Livebearing Fishes (Poeciliidae)* Prentice Hall, pp. 163–84.

Lambert, D. (1992a) 'Northern Rio Panuco swordtails Part 1' *Aquarist Pondkpr* **1992** (Mar.): 26–8.

Lambert, D. (1992b) 'The wild swordtails' *Aquarium Fish* **1992** (May): 50–58.

Lambert, D. (1992c) 'Northern Rio Panuco swordtails Part 2' *Aquarist Pondkpr* **1992** (Aug.): 100–102.

Lambert, D. (1992d) 'Swordmanship' *Practical Fishkeeping* **1992** (Aug.).

Lambert, D. & Lambert, P. (1988) '*Xiphophorus cortezi*' *Viviparous* **1988** (Jan.): 1–3.

Lambert, D. & Lambert, P. (1990) '*Xiphophorus xiphidium*' *Viviparous* **1990** (Jan.): 1–3.

Lambert, D. & Lambert, P. (1991a) '*Xiphophorus montezumae*' *Viviparous* **1990** (Jan.): 1–3.

Lambert, D. & Lambert, P. (1991b) '*Xiphophorus malinche*' *Viviparous* **1991** (Jul.): 1–3.

Lechner, P. & Radda, A. C. (1987) 'Revision des *Xiphophorus montezumae/cortezi*-Komplexes und Neubeschreibung einer Sunspezies. St Gallen, Switzerland' *Aquaria* **34**: 189–96.

Meek, S. E. (1904) 'The fresh water fishes from Mexico north of the Isthmus of Tehuantepic' *Field Columbian Mus. Publ., Zool. Ser.* **5**: 1–252.

Meffe, G. K. & Snelson, F. F. (1989) *Ecology and Evolution of Livebearing Fishes* Prentice Hall.

Meyer, M. K. & Schartl, M. (1980) 'Eine neue *Xiphophorus*-Art aus Vera Cruz, Mexico' *Senckenberg. Biol.* **60** (3–4): 147–51.

Meyer, M. K., Wichnath, L. & Forster, W. (1985) *Lebendgebarende Zierfische-Arten Der Welt* Mergus-Verlag.

Miller, R. .R. & Minckley, W. L. (1963) '*Xiphophorus gordoni*, a new species of platyfish from Coahuila, Mexico' *Copeia* **1963** (3): 538–46.

Norton, J. (1991a) 'Fancy livebearers. Part 1' *Freshwat. Mar. Aquarium* **1991** (Jun.): 8–13.

Norton, J. (1991b) 'Fancy livebearers. Part 2' *Freshwat. Mar. Aquarium* **1991** (Jul.): 48–51, 192.

Norton, J. (1991c) 'Fancy livebearers. Part 3' *Freshwat. Mar. Aquarium* **1991** (Sept.): 64–6.

Norton, J. (1991d) 'Fancy livebearers. Part 4' *Freshwat. Mar. Aquarium* **1991** (Nov.): 112–13.

Rauchenberger, M., Kallman, K. D. & Morizot, D. C. (1990) 'Monophyly and geography of the Rio Panuco Basin swordtails (genus *Xiphophorus*) with descriptions of four new species' *Am. Mus. Novit.* No. 2975: 41 pp.

Rosen, D. E. (1960) 'Middle-American poeciliid fishes of the genus *Xiphophorus*' *Bull. Fla St. Mus., Biol. Sci.* **5** (4): 57–242.

Rosen, D. E. (1979) 'Fishes from the uplands and intermontane basins of Guatemala: Revisionary studies and comparative geography' *Bull. Am. Mus. Nat. Hist.* **162** Art. 5: 332–74.

Rosen, D. E. & Bailey, R. M. (1963) 'The poeciliid fishes (Cyprinodontiformes). Their structure, zoogeography, and systematics' *Bull. Am. Mus. Nat. Hist.* **126** Art 1: 62–6.

Rosen, D. E. & Kallman, K. D. (1969) 'A new fish of the genus *Xiphophorus* from Guatemala, with remarks on the taxonomy of endemic forms' *Am. Mus. Novit.* No. 2379: 29 pp.

Schartl, M. & Schroeder, J. H. (1988) 'A new species of the genus *Xiphophorus*' *Senckenberg Biol.* **68**: 311–21.

Scott, P. W. (1987) *An Interpet Guide to Livebearing Fishes* Salamander Books Ltd.

Williams, J. E., Johnson, J. E., Hendrickson, D. A. Contreras-Balderas, S., Williams, J. D., Navarro-Mendoza, M., McAllister, D. E. & Deacon, J. E. (1989) 'Fishes of North America, endangered, threatened, or of special concern: 1989' *Fish. Bull. Am. Fish. Soc.* **14** (6): 2–20.

Vincent, W. F. & Forsyth, D. J. (1987) 'Geothermally influenced waters' In: A. B. Viner (ed) *Inland Waters of New Zealand*, Science Information Publ. Centre, Dept. Sci. and Indust. Res., Wellington, New Zealand, pp. 349–77.

CONVERSION TABLE

Length

1 mm	=	0.039 in
1 cm	=	0.394 in
1 m	=	$\begin{cases} 3.281 \text{ ft} \\ 1.094 \text{ yd} \end{cases}$
1 km	=	0.621 mile

Area

1 cm^2	=	0.155 sq. in
1 m^2	=	1.196 sq. yd
1 ha	=	2.471 acre
1 km^2	=	0.386 sq. mile

Volume

1 cm^3	=	0.061 cu. in
1 m^3	=	1.308 cu. yd

Capacity

1 ml	=	0.035 fl. oz
1 l	=	$\begin{cases} 35.211 \text{ fl. oz} \\ 1.760 \text{ pt} \\ 0.220 \text{ gal} \end{cases}$

Note:

1 l	=	$\begin{cases} 2.113 \text{ US pt} \\ 0.264 \text{ US gal} \end{cases}$

Weight

1 g	=	0.0353 oz
1 kg	=	2.205 lb
1 t	=	0.984 ton

Temperature

To convert °Centigrade to °Fahrenheit multiply by 9/5 and add 32.

Water Hardness

1°Clark	=	14.3 p.p.m. calcium carbonate
1°dH	=	17.9 p.p.m. calcium oxide

To convert °dH to °Clark multiply by 0.56.

Index

Page references in italic refer to line illustrations, and in bold to colour plates.